THE BOOK OF THISTLES

To Scarlett

Noëlle Janaczewska

25. 10. 2017

Noëlle Janaczewska is a playwright, poet and essayist. Much of her work deals with history's gaps and silences, focusing on people, plants, creatures and events which have been overlooked or marginalised in official records. Noëlle's work has been produced, broadcast and published throughout Australia and overseas, and in 2014 she received a prestigious Windham Campbell Prize from Yale University for her body of work as a dramatist. Closer to home her plays have won the Queensland Premier's Literary Award (*Mrs Petrov's Shoe*), the Playbox-Asialink Playwriting Competition and the Griffin Playwriting Award (*Songket*). The recipient of 7 AWGIE Awards (3 for radio nonfiction works and 4 for drama) and a University of Queensland Creative Fellowship (2012/2013), recent productions include: *Good With Maps* (Siren Theatre Company, Sydney 2016), *Teacup in a Storm* (The Q/Joan Sutherland Performing Arts Centre, Sydney 2016), *The History of the Single Girl* and *The Other Polish Explorer* for ABC Radio National in 2015, and the performance essays *Blasted Island - Nauru's backstory* for the Sydney Opera House 2014 Festival of Dangerous Ideas and *The Hannah First Collection, 1919-1949* for the Zendai Museum of Modern Art in Shanghai. Noëlle is an Adjunct Professor in the School of Communication and Arts at the University of Queensland.

THE BOOK OF THISTLES

NOËLLE JANACZEWSKA

First published in 2017 by
UWA Publishing
Crawley, Western Australia 6009
www.uwap.uwa.edu.au
UWAP is an imprint of UWA Publishing
a division of The University of Western Australia

National Library of Australia Cataloguing-in-Publication entry

Creator: Janaczewska, Noëlle, author.
Title: The book of thistles / Noëlle Janaczewska.
ISBN: 9781742588049 (paperback)
Subjects: Australian literature
Culture.
Home.
Emigration and immigration.

Design by Ten Deer Sigh
Printed by Mcphersons Printing Group
Cover image: courtesy Slava Gerj/BarbaraDiniz www.shutterstock.com

This project has been assisted by the Australian
Government through the Australia Council, its arts
funding and advisory body.

CONTENTS

OUTLIERS

ACKNOWLEDGEMENTS

The Book of Thistles was researched and written with a New Work grant from the Literature Board of the Australia Council for the Arts and an Eric Dark Flagship Fellowship (literary non-fiction) from The Writers' House.

Earlier versions of 'Hardheads & woolly thinking' and 'Darwin's thistles – a cautionary tale' were published in 2013 in the journals *Text* (Special Issue 18: *Nonfiction Now*) and *Mapping South: Journeys in South-South Cultural Relations* respectively.

'How to eat a thistle' and 'Eat more thistles!' were presented in live form as performance essays at the 2013 *Australian Gastronomy Symposium* in Newcastle and at the 2015 *Food & Words* festival in Sydney. Thanks to the curators of the Symposium and to Barbara Sweeney for inviting me to present at those events.

Thanks to the many librarians and archivists who helped me. At the State Libraries of New South Wales, Victoria, Tasmania and South Australia; at the State Records Authority of New South Wales and the State Records Office of Western Australia; at the British Library, at Yale University's Beinecke and Stirling Memorial Libraries, and elsewhere.

I couldn't have written this book without the National Library of Australia's Trove and the Biodiversity Heritage Library. Both provide free digital access to anyone with an internet connection. Long may they thrive.

Many thanks to Terri-ann White and the team at UWA Publishing, to editor Kelly Somers and to my agent Anthony Blair at Cameron Creswell for their various and much appreciated contributions to *The Book of Thistles*.

Thanks to my fellow 7-ON Playwrights (Donna Abela, Vanessa Bates, Hilary Bell, Verity Laughton, Ned Manning and Catherine Zimdahl) for their ongoing support and encouragement.

And finally, huge thanks to my partner, writer and filmmaker Kathryn Millard, for her critical insights, her intellectual imagination and for keeping me on an even keel. This book is for her.

INTRODUCTION

Thistles made my world larger.

The Book of Thistles is part accidental memoir, part environmental history and part exploration of the performative voice on the page. I come from a theatre background. And I'm a playwright whether I'm writing drama or non-fiction, a script, a poem or an essay.

Why thistles?

100 Plants that Almost Changed the World, *Western Civilization in Fifty Plants* – thistles don't appear in books with titles like these. They're considered neither charismatic nor history-shaping. Yet in Australia, and at different times in other countries too, thistles were hugely important.

I'm not a botanist. Although I now know a lot more about the subject than I did when I began this project, *The Book of Thistles* is about the cultural and social life of thistles. It's about the historical dramas played out between *Homo sapiens* and thistlekind, and how small, unrelated facts, if you take note of them, have a way of becoming connected.

I'm interested in unaccompanied language. In collage. In reveries and writings which switch register and jump-cut across genres. In literature not only as storytelling, but also as a form of thinking. That's why I love commonplace books and those eighteenth and nineteenth-century miscellanies in which scholars and curious amateurs exchanged ideas, knowledge, jests, journalism and random findings. Literature and scientific inquiry were dealt with in the same publication, so you might see a sonnet next to an article about geology, tips for growing vegetables alongside theological exposition.

Towards the end of my thistle project I reread Geoff Dyer's *Out of Sheer Rage (Wrestling with D.H. Lawrence)* and I found this wonderful quote: 'Spare me the drudgery of systematic examinations and give me the lightning flashes of those wild books in which there is no attempt to cover the ground thoroughly or reasonably.'

Yes!

Because of their variety, and the option of anonymous authorship, miscellanies were also places where more submerged voices could speak and where less orthodox forms of writing could be read. Given my preoccupation with history's gaps and silences, with the experiences of women, migrants and the marginalised, this struck a chord.

The word 'thistle' refers to a large and widespread group of plants. Several hundred species within the Asteraceae family, plus a bunch of other plants we call thistles – even though technically, botanically, they're not. Google 'thistles' and many of the sites will tell you how to get rid of them. Dig a little deeper, however, and from this weedy territory other narratives begin to emerge.

The thistle's disruptive tendencies appealed to me. Vagabond plants, sure, but also citizens of everywhere. 'They are perhaps the wildest of wild plants; the very embodiment of freedom and independence', wrote Flora A. Gordon in *The Journal of the School Nature Study Union* from 1916.

So I decided to put thistles centre-stage. Not background to important events, but offering an alternative focus of their own. Not to tell a single story, but to layer multiple possible stories.

And into the stories of thistles, I've interwoven snippets – facts and fictions – from my own life. Not only because I wanted to create a polyvocal text, but also because I wanted to understand the pull of this plant, the pull of the biota I grew up with, and the experience of being a migrant in a new land. I wanted to understand why I often felt untethered in my adopted homeland.

Because plants are immobile they make us think about place. *The Book of Thistles* is as much about place as it is about plants.

How do we locate a cultural home when 'home' is not one place?

NAMES

YELLOW MELANCHOLY

I

Yellow melancholy is a thistle.

It's the common name for *Cirsium erisithales*, and it was this plant, with its poetic and intriguing name, that triggered my interest in thistles. I came across it a few years ago, in a 1974 field guide, *The Wild Flowers of Britain and Northern Europe*, during a fugue of creative and career uncertainty that was speeding towards depression. I was looking through random books, looking for direction I suppose, when I chanced upon yellow melancholy on page 244, and felt my spirits lift.

I turned the page.

There was a second melancholy, this one with magenta flowers.

Unlike its yellow namesake, *Cirsium heterophyllum* is a British native. A northern and highland thistle that favours cool, moist conditions, it dots hayfields, verges and stream banks. Recent moves from pasture to silage, however, and the micromanagement of roadsides have led to a decline in their population.

Outside the United Kingdom, the melancholy thistle thrives in many upland parts of Europe, as does the rarer yellow melancholy. Neither species is present in Australia. My sober, environmentally responsible self cheers their absence, but there is a wild corner of me that regrets it.

*

Before Australia, I lived in London, and before that, in southern England, whose melancholy equivalent is the closely related meadow thistle, *Cirsium dissectum*. Like their melancholy kindred, these thistles have decreased in number and for similar reasons. The meadow thistle is vulnerable when its habitat is 'improved'. When its favoured fen and damp grasslands are drained and fertilised. Especially the latter. For many wildflowers the application of bulk chemical fertiliser has the same effect as a dose of weedkiller.

By contrast with most thistle species, the meadow and melancholies are characterised as wildflowers rather than weeds. 'The most gracious and benevolent of its tribe', was how conservationist and social reformer Henry S. Salt described what he called the mountain thistle – one of *C. heterophyllum*'s vernacular identities. He bemoaned 'the insolence of the passers-by, who knowing not what they do, maltreat it as if it were some vulgar pest of the fields, a thing to be hacked at and trampled on'.

The Call of the Wildflower, 1922.

The melancholy differs, too, in other respects.

Not only is it less invasive than many thistle species, it's also spineless. And as English illustrator and naturalist F. Edward Hulme put it, 'a thistle without this armature seems a thing contrary to nature'. Hulme's five-volume *Familiar Wild Flowers*, published on the hinge of the nineteenth and twentieth centuries, contains one of the longest entries I've found. A full five pages of text and pictures devoted to the melancholy thistle.

*

Relatively little may have been written about the melancholy thistle, but vast seas of ink have been spilled on the subject of melancholy per se. For hundreds of years it has taken centre-stage – for playwrights, poets and philosophers.

'My dusky, sullen foe' in the words of poet and dramatist Anne Finch (1661–1720).

A 'luxurious gloom of choice' for Wordsworth.

While Kierkegaard, through a matryoshka of invented characters, described it as 'the most faithful mistress I have known'.

It has been called many things: acedia, the English malady, green sickness.

Ascribed to many things: an excess of spleen, demonic forces, the influence of the planet Saturn.

The one constant is that melancholy eludes easy definition.

Robert Burton, author of that huge seventeenth-century tome *The Anatomy of Melancholy*, devoted his life to understanding melancholy in all its multifarious incarnations, but if you're daunted by ploughing through a thousand-plus pages, Shakespeare's *As You Like It* offers this tongue-in-cheek short cut:

> 'I have neither the scholar's melancholy, which is
> emulation, nor the musician's, which is fantastical,
> nor the courtier's, which is proud, nor the
> soldier's, which is ambitious, nor the lawyer's,
> which is politic, nor the lady's, which is nice, nor
> the lover's, which is all these: but it is a
> melancholy of mine own…'

By the time Freud coupled melancholy with loss in his 1917 essay 'Mourning and melancholy', the medicalisation of mental disorders was underway. Depression had entered the psychological lexicon and would soon eclipse melancholia.

Although melancholy seems a natural part of being human, I wonder if different cultures have their own shades of it? Perhaps it's no coincidence that some of the most difficult to translate words orbit around melancholy.

The German *Weltschmerz*.

The Portuguese *suadade*.

The Korean *han*.

And the Polish żal, a three-letter word with a score of meanings that crops up in just about every account of Chopin's life and music. A constellation of lament and longing, regret and rancour, frustrated patriotism and flashes of rage.

In England I had what we now call a portfolio or 'slash career': I was a community worker / arts administrator / office cleaner / sociology researcher / feral performer. In Australia I became a playwright. Migration gave me a new life in writing – it may even have been a prerequisite. My theatre writing grew out of a nomadic outlook and my reality as an immigrant in a nation of immigrants.

It thrived on journeys between different cultures and geographies. And the sorrowful and comic baggage that accompanies the soul on these crossings.

II

There are a few theories flying around about how the melancholy thistle acquired its adjective. The most popular explanation I've come across is that it was used to treat melancholy. According to the Doctrine of Signatures, if a plant's shape or properties resembled a part of the human body, it could be used to treat said body part's ailments. Although the roots of the philosophy go back to classical Greece and had been known to healers and apothecaries since that time, the Doctrine gained sway in the sixteenth century with the notion that God had given His creations signatures or signs to advertise their purpose.

It was an age in which similarity and look-alike played important roles in the organisation of knowledge.

Seventeenth-century herbalist Nicholas Culpeper took the drooping flower heads as the plant's 'signature' and recommended the 'Decoction of the Thistle in Wine being drunk, expels superfluous Melancholy out of the Body, and makes a man as merry as a Cricket'. In his opinion it is 'the best Remedy against all Melancholy Diseases'.

Although you have to wonder how much of the cure came from the thistle and how much from the alcohol.

The hanging-head story has been widely circulated and reproduction has given it the patina of authority. Yet in the sketches and photographs I've seen the stems are straight, the blooms erect. Barely a sag in sight, they appear anything but melancholy. The Culpeper explanation may well be the most likely one, but there are other contenders. A UK wildflower website, for example, tells a different tale: because the stalks branch only occasionally, the majority of plants offer a solitary, and thus melancholy, inflorescence.

*

I've seen neither of the melancholy thistles in real life. Only images in books and online. So when, during a visit to my mother's, I stumbled on a stand of them in the Goff's Oak local library, my curiosity was pricked. Here's the entry in *Flora of Hertfordshire*: 'A small colony of this species was established for a while following deliberate introduction to Meesden Green in the early 1980s. 13 plants were recorded in 1986.'

Almost twenty-five years later I knew the chance of finding those melancholy specimens was remote. *C. heterophyllum* may be a British native, but not this far south. Nevertheless, it was a tantalising snippet and I needed excursions and activities to entertain my elderly mother. I looked up Meesden on the map, assessed it to be about a forty-minute drive away and, a few days later, off we set.

But first a detour.

Meesden is in Hertfordshire, as is Goff's Oak, where I grew up and my mother still lives. One of England's 'home counties', Hertfordshire is a chalk and clay landscape bound by Essex to the east, Cambridgeshire to the north and London to the south.

For John Betjeman it was a place of 'mildly undistinguished hills'.

For me it was a Lego-scape of semi-detached houses, ring roads and mind-numbing boredom.

I left as soon as I could. And for a long time I didn't look back.

Goff's Oak lies in the bottom southeast corner of Hertfordshire in what is officially designated Green Belt. It's an area of not-quite-outer-suburban London that retains remnants of countryside – albeit scrappy countryside. Steel fences, light industry and retail barns scar the fields, but fields still exist.

Our route from Goff's Oak to Meesden, which is in the northeast of the county, took us up the A10. The scenery changed as we drove north and became positively picturesque after we turned off the main road. Villages laced together by winding lanes: Braughing, Green End, Dassels, Hare Street, then the B1038 to Brent Pelham where, my mother informed me, a notorious murderer cut up his wife and fed her to the pigs.

*

Heatwaves and dry spells, when municipal lawns reduce to dust, send me straight back to the northern hemisphere. In the midst of a Sydney summer, when the city cools off at the beach, I cool off with a dive into nostalgia. For the reality of a colder climate, and the fantasy of a place called Television England. Those crime-ridden villages where everyone has time for a cup of tea and a chat before they stab each other in the back. My *New Oxford Dictionary of English* actually defines a subsense of nostalgia as 'the evocation of these feelings or tendencies [a sentimental longing or wistful affection for the past] especially in commercialized form: *an evening of TV nostalgia*'.

Thanks in part to digital technology, nostalgia has jumped the picket fence – or privet hedge or dry-stone wall – to run rampant.

Facebook reconnects old school friends.

eBay sells retro-chic.

PhotoShop can brighten up the past or sepia-tint the present.

And every second documentary is about the heroes of World War I or II.

The village of Meesden ticks all the Television England boxes. No cow would dare shit on the road here. It's all well-kept cottages, big houses behind screens of established trees, a veneer that appears tranquil…perhaps deceptively so. At any moment we could cut to the scene where Miss Marple or Inspector Whoever announces there's been a murder at the vicarage.

In 1977 local historian Lionel M. Munby described Meesden as 'a parish of 1008 acres in the centre of countryside typical of northeast Hertfordshire…The undulating plateaux are broken by many small streams; the country is wooded and attractive in a low key'.

It hadn't changed much.

It was a mild September day. An Indian summer, my mother claimed, but there were hints the seasons were changing. England has few trees which turn red; the autumn palette here is yellow, amber and subtleties of brown.

I parked the car. My mother opted to stay put with a magazine and Thermos, while I set off with camera and notebook in search of the melancholy thistles. The roadside verges were beginning to look dishevelled. Tattered docks, mousey-smelling herb-Robert and thick clusters of thistles – not melancholy, but sturdy spear and creeping thistles. Both native species, the spears were still in bloom but the creeping ones were already gone to seed, their lilac flowers releasing clouds of down.

This was arable land, the soil turned regularly by machine blades. I stood in the field and felt the past steal up behind me, not in chronological narrative, but seesawing all over the place.

The Italian prisoners of war who stayed on and became market gardeners.

Anglo-Saxons clearing valleys and wildwood for agriculture.

Third-form history lessons, Mr Haywood explaining how the Enclosure Acts transformed the landscape, impoverished small farmers, and were a 'push' factor in emigration to the New World.

*

The trouble with nostalgia is that it not only rose-tints the past, but freeze-frames it as well. It detaches events and memories, refashions them as generic rather than specific, then sells them back to us as heritage.

Heritage.

There's a word to draw the sting from what farm labour really meant. When people lived on the brink of poverty, and illness, unemployment, even bad weather, could render them destitute. England may have smoothed out its rustic edges with gastro pubs and Jane Austen festivals, but you can still read a whole Bible of sorrows in these fields hemmed by ditches and banks of thistles.

*

A common is what was left after all the private land had been enclosed. Greens are smaller commons and the pair are survivors of old grassland.

Hertfordshire has a lot of greens and places with Green in their name.

Meesden Green, where the melancholy thistles of 1986 were sighted, was a patch of sward trimmed with a few trees and a public phone box I assumed was decorative rather than functional. Across the road was a small 'Nature Reserve (No Horses Thank You)' administered by the parish council. I examined both for melancholy thistles and, in an unmown strip of assorted grasses and wayside plants, discovered what I thought might indeed be *C. heterophyllum*. I'm no botanist, so I needed photographs to compare with references back at my mother's house. I was moving in for a close-up when ——

'Can I help you with something?' A resident from one of the ritzy properties overlooking the Green had spied me from her window and come to investigate. 'Are you from the council?'

I explained that I was looking for melancholy thistles.

She suggested I visit St Mary's at the other end of the village.

I reiterated my mission.

She gave directions to the church.

I hung around and took a few more photos while Mrs Neighbourhood Watch kept her eye on me and tried her best to herd me off her patch.

Something about that exchange made me feel a tremendous affinity with thistles. Not so much the melancholy, but all those thistles classified as weeds. Unwelcome squatters, vulgar pests and trash, the lot of us.

III

To everything there is a season…a time to plant and, when the leaves fall, a time for melancholy reflection. The season of mists and mellow fruitfulness is popular with poets, be they nineteenth-century Romantics or writers of Korean *sijo*, a lyric verse form that shares a partial ancestry with Japanese haiku and tanka. Melancholy flourished among the Romantics with their emphasis on subjectivity, but the gloomiest autumn poem I know is Dante Gabrielle Rossetti's *Autumn Song*, when 'the soul feels like a dried sheaf'. By contrast, many writers of *sijo* liked to counterpoint their autumnal melancholy with humour:

'Don't laugh at an old fisherman; he's there in every painting.'

The Fisherman's Calendar by Yun Seon-do, 1651.

But it's not only poets whose encounters with the natural world are coloured by melancholy. There's a genre of books and non-fiction films I've dubbed 'green melancholy'. Parables of ecological doom that go something like this: once was Eden, we stuffed up, we're still stuffing up, ergo things are going to get worse.

One position at the more vivid end of the green spectrum is that the environmental problems of today began thousands of years ago with the birth of agriculture. The clearing of indigenous vegetation to cultivate selected crops required a settled community, which over time led to urbanisation, dramatic population increase and all the attendant complications of energy generation, food security and waste disposal.

To me this is a Canute-like stance. We can't turn back the tide. And if you follow the logic of that argument, as American historian William Cronon does in *Uncommon Ground: Rethinking the Human Place in Nature*, then 'it is hard not to reach the conclusion that the only way human beings can hope to live naturally on earth is to follow the hunter gatherers back into the wilderness'.

*

Nostalgia and melancholy share many traits. At various points in history the ideas have overlapped and in contemporary speech we use the terms interchangeably, almost synonymously. Before it entered the domain of medicine, melancholy was a cast of mind that affected artists and intellectuals. Nostalgia's trajectory went in the opposite direction. In the seventeenth century it was considered a curable disease, and the first identified sufferers of this new syndrome were displaced people. Soldiers away from home.

It was still deemed an illness almost a century later, when Joseph Banks wrote in his journal that the crew of the *Endeavour* 'were now pretty far gone with the longing for home which the Physicians have gone so far as to esteem a disease under the name of Nostalgia'. Banks himself was unaffected, buffered by mental employment, which was, he reckoned, the best defence.

*

Despite the simplification of its landscape, Meesden and its environs remain the most rural part of Hertfordshire. It still fits Oliver Rackham's definition of 'ancient countryside', a geography of hamlet and coppice, low-sunk roads, public footpaths and isolated farms nestled in the lee of hills.

The day of our visit the hedgerows and verges were a mass of plants grumbling for sun and air. Heavy with elderberries, rosehips and a sour oval fruit my mother called a bullace.

Yellow melancholy thistles flower over summer and into early autumn, the regular melancholies in July and August.

It was mid-September when I went to Meesden, which meant the specimens I saw were either late-bloomers or not melancholy thistles at all. This turned out to be the case. My thistles were knapweeds.

Same family, different species.
Bracts pitch-brown
and brambly against my fingertips.
The obvious question
was it only thistles I was looking for that day?

For a whole bunch of reasons, my identity as a playwright was in flux. The dialogue was slipping away, so to speak. In the short term, I needed a way to roll my mind off its melancholy axis. Longer term, I needed purpose, and a more robust connection with the country I once called home.

IV

Yellow melancholy was first described by Nikolaus Joseph von Jacquin, but not classified as *Cirsium erisythales* until 1769. The *erisithales* bit of its name comes from the Greek *erithalis*, meaning luxuriant.

Although the yellow and magenta melancholies both favour elevated habitats, they are different species of thistle, not alternate hues of the same one. Here's a handful of gleaned facts about *C. erisithales*:

It likes to live above five hundred metres, in rivulets and rocky places, and will sometimes hybridise with other *Cirsiums*.

Its leaves are the shape and texture we typically associate with thistles, lobed and prickly. Foliage is sparse on the upper third of the stem.

In *Twelfth Night* Viola describes how passion unspoken festers in 'a green and yellow melancholy'.

And just to confuse matters, yellow melancholy is occasionally pink.

*

I can't entirely explain why that first encounter with yellow melancholy on page 244 of *The Wild Flowers of Britain and Northern Europe* so cheered me, but I can speculate...

C. erisithales is not a terribly prepossessing plant, but it has the most evocative name, a name that recalls the poetic tradition which informs so much English nature writing and not only nature writing, but landscape history, too. W. G. Hoskins began his influential 1955 book *The Making of the English Landscape* not with statistics or theoretical exposition, but with Wordsworth and the remark that 'poets make the best topographers'.

Yellow melancholy recharged my interest in the plant

realm and our human interactions with it, a longstanding interest but one which had lain dormant a while. It suggested possibilities. New ecologies of exploration and research.

From this first encounter unfurled a fascination with thistles, with those plants we brand as weeds, and with the histories of environments both physical and fictional.

I started to see thistles as a kind of text, multilayered, multilingual, full of uneasy but exciting reminders of the expanse of untamed nature just over the horizon. Legacies of the wild that haunts civilisation.

'The landscape is like a historic library of 50,000 books', according to Oliver Rackham. 'Many were written in remote antiquity in languages which have only lately been deciphered; some of the languages are still unknown.'

The History of the Countryside, 1995.

*

Time turns things a different colour. Not only plants. Memories and associations can slow-brew from neutral to mellow gold.

On that note, let's backstitch a moment. What happened to those melancholy thistles of 1986?

The seeds are wind dispersed, so occasional long-distance scatterings do occur, but not this far from home. Did they find the local climate inhospitable and die out after a few cycles? Or did some Meesden resident on a tidy binge uproot them by mistake?

Unlike knapweed, the leaves of *C. heterophyllum* have a silvery underside, hence another of the plant's common names: fish belly. Other melancholy monikers include 'the great English soft' or 'gentle thistle'.

Although the melancholy thistle had been a familiar feature for centuries, it was not officially recorded until the sixteenth century, after a London physician called Thomas Penny told the pioneering French botanist Charles de l'Écluse of its 'discovery' in Ingleborough in North Yorkshire in 1581. De l'Écluse labelled the thistle *Cirsium britannicum*.

Botanical taxonomy is a minefield. Plant names followed by a stutter of abbreviations, dates, parentheses and credits.

In a 1938 article, biologist H. K. Airy-Shaw untangled the melancholy thistle's Latin lineage. Here's a brief and very partial synopsis:

After several variations on the theme of *Cirsium Britannicum*, Linnaeus described *Carduus helenioïdes* and *Carduus heterophyllus* in 1753. Variant spellings aside, this provoked a long debate about whether *helenioïdes* and *heterophyllus* were one and the same or two distinct species. Until James Edward Smith, founder of the Linnean Society of London and friend of Joseph Banks, wrote that *Carduus helenioïdes* was not only a quite different plant, but 'a stranger to our island'. After which the name all but disappeared from surveys of British flora.

Until the internet reinstated it. Now so much material is available electronically, the *helenioïdes* tag is again cropping up.

*

Recent studies suggest the capacity to remember may not be confined to animals. Higher plants may also have a form of memory. Like us, they're shaped by what happens to them and alter their responses to future events accordingly. It isn't conscious memory of course; those spear thistles in Meesden weren't standing there reminiscing about the night frosts of January 2009. But a team of scientists based at Rothamsted Research (in Hertfordshire) says there is evidence that stressors such as drought, cold, fluctuating soil salinity, hostile fungi, insect plagues or bacteria may be remembered in a vegetative kind of way.

The molecular mechanism by which plants store information is still being explored, but what I want to know is: If plants remember, can they also forget?

*

We drove back from Meesden via Nuthampstead. My mother wanted to see the abandoned World War II airfield. When it was closed or decommissioned or whatever it is that happens to old military installations, the runways were dug up and recycled, leaving only a landing strip for crop-spraying and other small aircraft. In the 1960s and '70s the village hit the public radar when it was shortlisted as a site for London's third airport.

I switched on the car radio. There was a Miles Davis track playing, an early one, from *Kind of Blue*. I often listen to jazz when I'm writing; its fugitive, elliptical forms bring new, non-linear shapes to my thoughts. I know this album well, so I upped the volume to relish Miles – sometimes celebratory, sometimes melancholy.

The sky was overcast and threatening rain by the time we reached the airfield.

The conifers in the background turned black.

The kids rehearsing their skateboard moves called it a day.

No one else was about, just the two of us and some sow thistles pushing along the perimeter.

My vision of Hertfordshire, of England, is a contradictory one.

Yes, to rushy streams, overarching trees,
the midnight snowfall that winter brings.
No, to a longish list of other things.

As a teenager I longed to escape my home county, where the traffic flowed in all directions and it was easy to find yourself funnelled onto a ring road, going round in circles, unable to find the exit.

Like one of those Escher drawings.

Overhead a flock of birds in V-formation followed their inner compass south, and I reminded myself that I did find a way out. Australia provided me that service it has afforded immigrants throughout its history. The opportunity to stop being who they were and start being who they wanted to be. An offer I took up with alacrity.

A few minutes later a plane crescendoed into earshot. Not an old Spitfire, but a Boeing 737. Stansted Airport is less than twenty kilometres from Nuthampstead. Miss Marple's sleuthing would be sound-tracked by the roar of a jet packed with holiday-makers en route to Ibiza.

It started to rain.

We were told to get off a dirt track because it belonged to somebody private.

Our tea was stone cold in its flask.

I drove us back to the twenty-first century, and a week later I flew home to Sydney.

Forget therapy and the prescription pad, let's return melancholy to artists, writers and thinkers. Not as the corrosive by-product of creative genius, but as an integral part of the human quest.

Back in Australia I searched a forest of references in an attempt to solve the mystery of the pendulous flower heads. I unearthed conflicting information, a lot of cutting and pasting of the same information, and no clear consensus. Nevertheless, a couple of the more reliable sources do state that, although the adult flowers are upright, the buds have a tendency to droop. When they stir in the wind they give the melancholy thistle its sad mien.

And hence the name that so captured my imagination.

SCOTCH THISTLES – THREE FAIRYTALES, TWO QUOTES & A LYRIC

Nearly a long time ago a trespasser barged into virgin bush. Actually, not so virgin. That was a myth dressed up in fancy Latin. Once ever after there was a thistle and nearly a long time ago, after ever such a long sea voyage, it arrived. In Australia. Why? Who can be sure? Some say accident. Others say design. In any case, it grew. God saw to that. And gardeners. And farmers with their sheep and groats. Officially this thistle was a mouthful of Latin: *Onopordum acanthium*. Unofficially it was cotton, heraldic or Scotch. Its flowers were. Words for purple: plum, mulberry, punky-pink. They weren't innocent, said the Powerful Men. They were a giant problem. Towering two-and-a-half, even three metres. Leaves long as your arm. If we didn't get them first the intruders would help themselves to the land's honey. Shamble paddocks. Throw their seeds around and have themselves a ceilidh at our expense. The Powerful Men took the high ground and talked clearances. Stars watched as they shunted clauses back and forth. Till compromise was firmly planted. And then with the help of law enforcement, weed managers and cauldrons' worth of herbicides, they arrested the offender's spread. No magic. Just a half-way happy ending and a wayward thistle sentenced to death. Heads chopped off. But still. As the stars keep their unbroken watch. There remains. In foreign fields. Corners of forever Scotland.

*

Nations rally behind their chosen plants. Japan's cherry blossom, the cedar of Lebanon, Canadian maple. The Scottish thistle. Everywhere you go in Scotland you find them. On beer mats, bracelets, business logos. A ubiquitous symbol. The English went roses. Scots went prickly. There were royal stanzas. *The Thrissil and the Rois* by William Dunbar celebrated the 1503 marriage of King James IV. There were legends from long-a-way back. Once upon a time, an ancient half-forgotten time when there was less noise, were Vikings. And a Viking raiding party launched a surprise attack on Scotland. Where the woods are cinematic. The way the story goes it was night and the clouds had starlight covered. The invaders crept towards the unsuspecting. Barefoot. Not a sound to stir the sleeping Scots. Until —— Ouch! One of the marauders stepped on a thistle. His cry alerted the Scottish army. Who defended their territory and saw off the would-be invaders.

Once, twice, many times. Botanists have tried to affix a species to the symbol. *Onopordum acanthium*, the cotton thistle often called Scotch is neither a Highland nor a Lowland native. A sporadic wilding. (A changeling in Australia and other away-from-home places. But that's a story for another day.) Spear thistle is a more likely contender for the title. The Scottish thistle. Commonplace and undoubtedly indigenous. But thistles in context. Belong to heath, hayfield and happenstance. Perk up ditch-sides with their luminous magenta. The Scottish thistle is an emblem. Scientific identification isn't the point. 'The point is in the prickle', insists J. H. Crawford in *Wild Flowers of Scotland* (1897). 'All this pother has been raised by species-mongers...If we have any preference, it is for the most bristly-looking.'

*

Far away and not so long ago there was a massive hedge. Was there a witch behind it? Probably. Every castle has one. Even semi-suburban castles. It was a mixed-up hedge. Hawthorn. Hazel. Umbels of cow parsley. And huge cotton thistles with ghosty-white stems. Everyone knows Sleeping Beauty. And the prick that sends the tale spinning into grim territory. Once upon a time when merchandise was still a noun. I'm sure you know what happened. Princes came to try their luck. They all got stuck. Until the clock struck one hundred years. The spell snapped. And the final prince penetrated. The princess awoke. Dada-da, they got married and lived sensibly ever after. I thought the royals were boring. The hedge was far more interesting than either of them. Closer to home I was forever dragging my brother and Sheila-from-number-twelve to the witchy hedge. The cotton thistles grew wide as well as tall. Nobody would dare their thorns. I made up stories. There were skeletal remains and other mysteries trapped inside that thistly undergrowth. My hands got bloody from reaching in. My imagination was buzzing like a wasp in a glass. Some stuff is complicated. Some is simple. The woman who lived alone behind the massive hedge was called Orla or Olga. Something like that. My mother started visiting her with jars of homemade jam and slices of veal and ham pie. My father was a quiet man in a pullover. He kept to himself. The hedge kept growing. I went back to school. Autumn trudged into winter and spring followed. New thistles shot up. Then suddenly one morning. Sad news Mum told us. Orla or Olga had passed away. What about the hedge? I raced down the road. Council workers arrived. With chainsaws. Hawthorn, hazel, cow parsley, thistles cut down to size. And as they disappeared so did the gothic goings-on. And the sorcery that we'd scared ourselves silly imagining. All that remained was a completely ordinary little house. A For Sale sign planted where the cotton-thistly hedge once grew.

*

'Another unlucky importation was the Scotch thistle, which a patriotic Scotch lady near here planted in her garden and which, like most of its compatriots, took so kindly to the country that it grows everywhere.'

Letter from Rachel Henning to her sister in England. Bathurst, New South Wales, July 1861.

'The invasion of the New World by Scotch thistles was due to a curious accident.

Some sixty or seventy years ago emigrants' outfitting shops in the neighbourhood of Liverpool Docks suddenly developed a big trade in thistle-down, used for making mattresses for the use of emigrants.

From Boston, New York, and Philadelphia the emigrants passed inland with their mattresses, which eventually wore out, and, being thrown on the farmyard rubbish heap, provided formidable centres of dispersal of a plague of thistles.'

The Telegraph, Brisbane, August 1926.

Mattresses are the medium in another origin story.

'The *Scotch Thistle* is a very troublesome weed, along our sea-coast. The people say, a Scotch minister brought with him a bed stuffed with thistledown, in which was contained some seed. The inhabitants, having plenty of feathers, soon turned out the down, and filled the bed with feathers. The seed coming up, filled that part of the country with Thistles.'

A brief account of those Plants that are most troublesome in our pastures and fields, in Pennsylvania... by John Bartram. Included with his letter to Philip Miller, June 1758.

*

The Scotch thistle has grown
into a song.
It could happen
to any plant.

Where the landscape unwinds
and light falls into light
there among the stock and oats
lacquered in legend and anecdotes
the Scotch thistle has grown
into a song.

Nothing too anthem-like
no bagpipes please
no Auld Lang Syne.

A Celtic lullaby
or ballad lost
in its own heartbreak.

Where gloved hands hold hymn books
and weather is epic
there among the stock and oats
lacquered in legend and anecdotes
the Scotch thistle has grown
into a song.

JOHN PARKINSON'S THISTLES

From 'Thistles and thornie plants' described by John Parkinson in *The Theatre of Plants (or an Herball of Large Extent)*, published in 1640. Parkinson was apothecary to King James I and later Royal Botanist to King Charles I.

The yellow jagged meadow thistle.
Another soft melancholy thistle.

The fish thistle with a broad yellow flower.
——with broad reddish flowers.

Round headed fish thistle.
The low fish thistle with winged stalks.

The cruel sharp thistle.
The true chameleon or changeable thistle without a stalk.

Our low wild carline thistle.
The pine apple thistle

The common ladies thistle.
Great milk thistle of a year.

The smallest globe thistle with the most prickly leaves.
The *French* supposed white thistle.

The gentler way thistle.
The asses cracking thistle.

The most prickly thistle.
The many headed thistle.

The small smooth bastard sea holly.
The gentle thistle with jagged leaves.

HARDHEADS & WOOLLY THINKING

A thistle is a thistle is sometimes a thistle in name only. So it is with creeping knapweed, otherwise known as hardhead thistles or just hardheads. Its Latin name is *Rhaponticum repens*. Although maybe not for much longer. Since the 2011 International Botanical Congress voted to allow plants in plain English.

Knapweeds as a tribe are robust and adaptable. Popular with insects. Close cousins of thistles, and equally cosmopolitan, they cover a lot of ground.

Common or black.

Greater and lesser.

Spotted.

Diffuse.

The species that interests me is the creeping one. Recognised by a host of signatures. As well as hardheads there's:

Poverty weed.

Russian knapweed.

Turkestan thistle.

In regional Queensland, funnel or thimble top ——

The list of local names goes on. A colloquial lexicon, part of the poetic ecosystem. A shared cultural endeavour that reaches back centuries.

My father was the king of lists. For Dad, making a list was almost as important as the task. A point of view I've come to share – even extend. Put something on my to-do list and quite often that's the end of it. Time passes and with it the imperative.

After my father died I found lists going back decades. Along with a huge collection of torches, camping lamps and spare batteries. A collection that spoke of his worries over power cuts and being left in the dark.

The mind's circuits recoil.

I was back in England, in the place I grew up. Dogleg lanes, secret pockets, odd-lit hollows, drifts of stories, grunge and gravel.

I'm skipping along, my small hand in Dad's grown-up one. We're out for a walk in the break between one downpour and the next, when everything is flung open. Oak trees shake out the light, rainwater sparkles in ditches. And Dad explains the wildlife along the way.

It got its name from the white down on its involucre, you said – although I doubt you used the word 'involucre'. See how big they are, and spherical, like ping-pong balls or tiny globes.

The woolly headed thistle towered above me, twice my height. A beanstalk of a plant.

'It has less the air of a native Plant of our country, than most others', declared *The Vegetable System* of 1762, where it is not only Woolly Headed but Bristly to boot.

They like roadsides and grassland, you told me. Areas not too neat and tidy.

Every bloom is a massive cupped handful. A pink so intense it could be shocking. I wonder how it got there; imagine wolves leaping out of library books and beans sprouting into giants overnight.

Arise über thistle, your roots are Latin, your origin fuzzy.

Creeping knapweed has its origins around the Caspian Sea, in the scrub and steppes of Central Asia. From where it has spread across the temperate world to become a major weed. The *Smithsonian* magazine labelled its spotted sibling 'a weed of mass destruction'. So rampant was the purple-flowered pest in some states that migrating elk changed course to avoid it.

We don't know exactly when or how creeping knapweed arrived in Australia. Best estimate is around 1900. Possibly, probably, introduced in consignments of imported seed-stock. It was recorded growing in Victoria in 1907, in southeast Queensland nine years later, and in South Australia by 1930. It's widespread across inland New South Wales.

The basic narrative goes something like this:

There was an outburst. A series of outbursts erupting from the rough ends and edges, from brush and paddock, yards and shoulders. In the pinch between spring's finale and midsummer, hardheads ran up to flower and ran wild.

'Had it not been for the war, with its consequent diversion of manpower from rural enterprise, the weed might easily have been eradicated and its spread to other districts prevented, but the six years of international conflict, when everyone's attention was focused mainly on the combat theatres, gave the weed every opportunity of undetected advance.'

The Chronicle, Adelaide, June 1946.

'The Weeds Adviser to the Department of Agriculture (Mr H. E. Orchard) said yesterday this weed was one of the most menacing of the State and most difficult to kill.'

The Adelaide Advertiser, January 1947.

Rewind a bit further and overseas infestations were retold in Australia as cautionary tales.

US authorities warn farmers about Russian knapweed

contamination 'following the promiscuous purchase of alfalfa (lucerne) seed from Turkestan'.

The Townsville Daily Bulletin, November 1914.

*

England in the early '70s was dull, dull, dull. Literally.

December 1970. Power workers banned overtime in pursuit of a wage claim. The lights went out. The government of the day banned the use of electricity for non-essential purposes. Christmas trees were stripped of their fairy lights. Our house plunged into chilly darkness.

That first week of blackouts the kitchen was transformed into a candle-lit war room where we tracked the dispute. Ads for emergency lighting sat on the table next to plates of sandwiches.

Dad panic-bought a dozen torches.

February 1972. The miners were on strike. More freezing weather. More power cuts. On the upside, evenings the electricity blinked off provided the perfect excuse:

The miners ate my homework, Miss.

Power to the miners!

The price of candles skyrocketed. Dad acquired several more torches.

Winter 1974. The miners worked-to-rule, the rest of the country worked a three-day week. Politicians urged us to switch off and save.

Newspapers predicted food shortages, public chaos, crisis on all fronts. Since he'd got into sociology Dad had been predicting the collapse of capitalism. But now it seemed immanent, he was annoyed.

The hardware shop refused to sell him any more torches. Wouldn't be fair to his other customers, the manager said. And my mother refused to queue in the cold to buy extra batteries.

It was dark, but Dad wanted to conserve his supply. So Mum arranged candles on the windowsill. Their flickering seized by the snow outside, magnified, and tossed into the air like fireworks.

*

What's in a name?

Latin was the lingua franca that let scientists and scholars speak to each other. But not any more. Plants will keep their double-barrelled Latin monikers, but the validating profiles can now be in English.

Actually, Latin isn't always the guarantee of precision and consistency we assume. Creeping knapweed was originally described by Linnaeus as *Centaurea repens* in 1763. *Centaurea* after the hybrid creatures of Greek mythology. And *repens*, a disposition to crawl. In 1838 the Swiss naturalist and avid classifier de Candolle placed it in the genus *Acroptilon*, where it remained until a different classification was proposed in 2006. Based on DNA analysis, researchers suggested that *Acroptilon* should be submerged in the genus *Rhaponticum*. Thus creeping knapweed became *Rhaponticum repens*.

Outside the botanical establishment most of us prefer a simpler ID: woolly headed thistle rather than *Cirsium eriophorum*. Names which log particular characteristics or habitats. Names redolent of superstitions and kids' games. There's a whole landscape of vernacular poetry out there.

The shift to English was prompted by the need to accelerate the cataloguing process for the estimated hundred thousand as-yet-unnamed species. Before they disappear off the face of the earth.

A rose by any other name might smell as sweet, but a plant

without a name has no advocate. No one to defend it from the forces of extinction, no one even to notice when it's gone. To give something a name is to begin a relationship with it.

Plus Latin is difficult, opaque. Spiked with arcane references.

The vernacular is about home turf and the story-seeds we carry with us.

Hardheads might be hard to grasp taxonomically. Not so in practice. Unlike thistles, the hardhead, all knapweeds in fact, are spineless.

Appearance-wise it's nothing special. Between forty and a hundred centimetres tall, leaves with a hint of grey, florets anywhere on the dusky pink to reddish-purple spectrum. These sit atop a tough receptacle that looks a bit like a miniature pineapple. Hence the hardhead tag.

Drought resistant and salt tolerant, creeping knapweed generally colonises disturbed terrain. Able to reproduce by root as well as seed, it forms dense patches. Inhibits the growth of adjacent vegetation by releasing toxins into the soil. Effectively clearing the ground for more of its own kind.

'In the fruitgrowing settlements of the Murray it has been known to send its roots right underneath a road, and to produce new top growth on the other side. A concrete irrigation channel several feet deep also proved ineffective as a barrier against the creeping advance.'
The Chronicle, Adelaide, June 1946.

You've got to admire, or at least respect, this plant's vigour and don't-mess-with-me attitude.

There's a report – it's that South Australian Weeds Adviser, the aptly named Mr Orchard again – about using electricity to control weeds. Field tests in California had apparently been successful in containing knapweed:

'The machine, known as the Electrovater, generates a very high voltage which is passed through rake-like electrodes to the weeds.'

The Burra Record, August 1948.

Nobody loves a hardhead thistle. Its tenure threatens the agricultural order. It pushes its way through dirt and crap, shrugs off pesticides and competitors to grab the sunlight. A plant 'at whose name the verse feels loath', as Shelley put it.

Words clash against hardheads. Their prevalence generates a kind of heated rhetoric. Sentences that bristle with razor wire.

Provide a label and you gather a body of thought.

From ideas pitched in theoretical registers discussion spreads into feelings about belonging, about displacement and ownership, about individual rights over the land. And the nature of change.

As a migrant to Australia from England, with my own anxieties about belonging and distance, I'm drawn to the story of this thistle look-alike.

A few years ago my partner and I rented a cottage in the Blue Mountains for a summer break. It had the classic holiday home inventory:

Mismatched china.

Jigsaws with missing pieces.

Random field guides – not to local nature, which could have been useful, but to the wildflowers of Great Britain.

Black nightshade.

Cow parsley.

Bittersweet.

I could recite their names in a way I couldn't Australian flora. Despite more than twenty years' residence. I was shocked. Then sad. It made me feel like – like one of those puzzles with lost pieces.

*

I was looking for a box to hold my father's stash of torches, thirty-nine in total, when I came across a typical list scribbled on the back of an envelope. It wasn't only the familiarity of his blue-biro handwriting, the minutiae of a life that was now irrefutably over, that brought tears to my eyes. And yes, made me smile, too. It was also the purpose of that list. Had those thoughts been completed? Those tasks accomplished? I envisioned other lists, scores of notes lurking in drawers or in the oily dusk of the garage.

My father's voice, his reasoning, his repartee, his grammatically correct emails, a detailed sense of his being came flooding back to me with that list.

It began in a curiously poetic register:

As the light crumbled over park benches
where they lay under newspapers ——
Then switched to the prosaic:
Pay the papers. Tick.
Confirm Friday. Tick.
Headway re parking.
Library – must pick up by 7. Underlined.

When did libraries get rebranded learning centres? A library is a noun with a history. A place where manifestos might be researched, sonnets composed, databases or rare volumes opened. Where the subplots are prolific. A place of serendipitous discoveries. Somewhere a recent immigrant might go to find a novel in her mother tongue.

A library invites, it suggests the wider world. A learning centre suggests – well, remedial education. Somewhere people are crafting stuff with raffia or plasticine.

My first library was a wooden shed. A matchbox of a building.

I learnt from the ancient one behind the desk that I was overdue. Fines needed to be paid before I could borrow my four books.

I didn't have any money.

Then you'll have to wait until you do, she snapped.

I was at that waiting age. Waiting for holidays. Waiting to go back to school. Waiting to be a teenager. Waiting for life to come to some kind of point, the way it came to a point on the printed page.

And now I'm going to stretch a point and cross-pollinate flashlights with thistles so I can mention the plant old texts dub torch thistle.

Another misnomer. In this case it is a cactus from Mexico. A candelabra-shaped species whose buds open for just a few hours once a year, on a night when there is a full or near-full moon.

Australia's relationship with hardhead thistles digs into a series of deeper, thornier questions.

About what we believe counts as responsible citizenship.

About evolving notions of national identity, the siting of frontiers, and how we relate to each other across our differences.

About deserving and undeserving nature. All those shades of green –

Legal.

Scientific.

Romantic.

Tragic.

*

I organised my father's effects. But it wasn't enough.

So a drizzly September afternoon I revisited the spot where we'd seen the woolly headed thistle and counted its swollen heads. It was long gone of course. A new estate in its place. Houses secured behind electronic gates.

In my mind the woolly headed thistle had grown to a dizzying height. Bloated, bulbous, it was a plant I suspected of sentience. A shapeshifter. A thistle more at home in Alice's Wonderland or Middle Earth. When your back was turned it might open an eye or move a limb.

It occupies a murky space. Where it's not clear which plants are weeds and which are not.

'By far the most specious of all our Thistles', according to the 1835 edition of *The Gardener's Dictionary*.

Have a closer look, Dad said, and lifted me up to thistle level so I could touch an inflorescence. I doubt he used that word either.

Clouds part, a crab apple tree drops its load. The scene is suddenly flush with colour and shadow-play.

I picture you in a museum, the past illuminated, where men of science wear their eternity.

Latin erected into names. Stumbled into steps. Fashioned into narrative.

Entrance. Exit. Lights out.

I didn't appreciate until I reignited my childhood interest in nature that by migrating to a different nature on the other side of the planet, I'd lost a connection. The thread by which you continue to weave a relationship with the place you came from before you came here.

'There scabious blue, and purple knapweed rise,
And weld and yarrow show their various dyes.'

That's from *Amoebaen Eclogues* by John Scott. Eighteenth-century poet and reformer.

Hardheads remind us that life doesn't always rhyme. Remind us that humans entering new environments tend to change them, often irrevocably. As indeed they change us.

But in their different ways, hardheads and woolly headed thistles suggest to me that maybe a part of being Australian is feeling a part of somewhere else.

RUSSIAN THISTLE

You are an icon. A legend. Tumbleweeds get thrown about. Many different plants claim that title: tumbleweed. But you are a star performer. Russian thistle, *Salsola kali*. A pretty name. You may have known the Latin of Linneaus. You may not. His sexual system. There was the usual. Rumours. Tittle-tattle. 1880 the US Department of Agriculture received word of a strange new plant growing in South Dakota. Someone shrugged. Someone made coffee. Someone filed the report. More rumours. Specimens, too. Washington sent a botanist to find out what the hell was going on out there. 1894 the year of Dreyfus and Coca-Cola sold in bottles. Votes for women in South Australia. A bulletin was published: *The Russian Thistle*. Zoom in for a close-up. 'The rapidity with which the Russian thistle has spread, both in infesting new territory and in thoroughly covering that already infested, far exceeds that of any weed known in America.' Some claimed you were a deliberate act. Of malice. Russian immigrants were to blame. With their contaminated flaxseed. Not true. You were an accidental. But your accent *is* Russian. On the Steppe they know you as leap-the-field. Are you Tolstoy's thistle from *Hadji Murad*? No. You're just playing the part of a thistle. Not even that. You're a stand-in. You're as much like a cabbage as you are a thistle. Critics' harsh words. You are a horror. Tempestuous. Bloody headed. Out of control. The end of the nineteenth century you made it to California. Hollywood. A regular feature. Westerns. Cowboys. Slide guitar. Scuff ruff rock and roly-poly. You are a survivor. *Outer Limits* and weirdo science. At ground zero you're first on the comeback trail. You survive meltdowns and ideology. Diffuse terrors. Skies the colour of pomegranates. You play fast and loose. Pushed about by wind. Thick-bristle Russian thistle. Your roots tap a million migrations. Who will blossom? Who will be clipped? Who will be sent screaming to a distant planet?

DARWIN'S THISTLES – A CAUTIONARY TALE

They must have been an extraordinary sight. Like a scene from a fairytale.

People described them.

Offered explanations, advanced theories, considered them as metaphors for human scrappiness.

Either way, they wrote about them. In English.

In Spanish, French and German.

Probably other languages as well.

Félix de Azara recorded them growing around houses and across pastureland. They were there, he explained, because man was there with his quadrupeds.

Cattle.

Horses.

Mules.

Probably other beasts as well.

Charles Darwin read Azara in French translation: *Voyages dans l'Amérique méridionale, depuis 1781 jusqu'en 1801*. He referenced Azara twenty-three times in *The Voyage of the Beagle*. Digitisation makes the count quick and easy.

Travelling between Bahia Bianca and Buenos Aires in the spring of 1833 Darwin observed mile upon mile 'covered by one mass of these prickly plants'. He was referring to the cardoon, sometimes called the artichoke thistle. Or, to give it its Latin binomial, *Cynara cardunculus*.

Thistles were intruders on the Pampas.

'Over the undulating plains, where these great beds occur, nothing else can now live. Before their introduction, however, the surface must have supported, as in other parts, a rank herbage. I doubt whether any case is on record of an invasion on so grand a scale of one plant over the aborigines.'

Darwin wasn't the first.

During his *Voyage to Buenos Ayres performed in the years 1817 and 1818 by order of the American Government*, H. M. Brackenridge mentioned 'great quantities of a species of thistle'.

In 1821 Alexander Caldcleugh 'traversed at least twenty leagues of them' on his *Travels in South America.*

W. P. Robertson coined the term 'thistleries' to describe what he and his brother saw: thistles 'extending their dominions on all sides…destined to become the last great vegetable usurpers on the whole Pampas'.

'So thick do these thistles grow to the southward', wrote John Miers, 'that the inhabitants of the northern parts can rely upon their security from Indian attacks, as the intervening district is rendered almost impassable by them'.

Lieutenant Charles Brand witnessed the burning of thistles to clear land in 1827. 'For miles was it to be seen blazing and marching majestically along the horizon, a wilderness of fire.'

While Thomas Woodbine Hinchcliffe lost his guide among 'the gigantic thistles of Entre Rios'.

There were lots of them.
Travellers, entrepreneurs, ex-military.
Some were men of science and ideas, like d'Orbigny and Darwin.

Others were men on a mission, penning handbooks to encourage European emigration to the New World.

They invariably mentioned thistles. They invariably paraphrased Captain Head's account of them, adding little grace notes here and there.

The thistles had a seasonal rhythm.

Captain Francis Bond Head detailed their cycle of growth and decay in *Rough Notes taken during some rapid journeys across the Pampas and among the Andes*. He assumed the enormous thistles he saw were indigenous, the product of 'an Omnipotent Creator'.

Darwin picked up on Captain Head's giant thistle.

Australian newspapers picked up on Captain Head's book. The fields of thistles he reported struck a particular chord.

'A sound mind, on beholding this dreary desert, would lament that art had not covered the soil with the various productions useful to man; our author is solely induced to reflect "upon the regularity and *beauty* of the vegetable world, when left to the wise arrangements of Nature". The *beauty* of an unvaried surface of one hundred and fifty miles of wild thistles, is beyond our conception.'

The Monitor, Sydney, July 1827.

*

I'm surrounded by mountains

of books and journals, technical studies, sketches and memoirs. Delivered from off-site storage.

My Spanish runs as far as two beers please and thanks for everything. So the volumes I'm reading are in English and French.

Mostly English.

Mostly with very long titles. Here's an example: *The States of the River Plate: their industries and commerce. Sheep-farming, sheep-breeding, cattle-feeding, and meat-preserving; employment of capital; land and stock, and their values; labour and its remuneration*, by William Latham, 1866.

I'm working in the Stirling Memorial Library at Yale University. My partner is here as a Visiting Fellow and I've tagged along. I like libraries and Yale has a fine collection of them.

It's the end of March and the campus dogwoods are in blossom.

The books I've requested are old, published in the nineteenth century. Their bindings are brittle and, despite my care turning pages, corners crumble and fall to the ground like confetti. Or blossom.

Darwin got it wrong. Kind of. He recognised that there were two types of thistle in the Pampas: the cardoon and the 'great thistle', but this latter species puzzled him. 'Do you know what is the giant thistle of the Pampas?' he asked his mentor, John Henslow.

We now know that the 'great thistles' were variegated thistles, alias milk thistle, cabbage thistle, St Mary's thistle and blessed thistle – although *Silybum marianum* wasn't considered a blessing by everyone.

William MacCann, who crossed the Pampas in the 1840s, refers to three varieties.

The gigantic thistle of the plains.

An edible thistle.

The ague thistle, which is poisonous.

MacCann's *Two Thousand Miles' Ride through the Argentine Provinces* was probably inspired by Captain Head's much reprinted 1826 book, and his gigantic thistle was almost certainly the variegated thistle.

*

In 1789 Governor King wrote to Joseph Banks requesting seeds for the newly established colony at Sydney Cove. His wish list included a plant he called *Carduus benedictus*. This was probably the thistle botanists now call *Silybum marianum* and it was most likely wanted for medicinal purposes.

Half a century later, it was a weed.

In New South Wales.

In Victoria.

In South Australia.

And in Tasmania.

'Every garden and spare spot about town is overgrown with thistles. If some steps of the kind we now recommend be not taken in a few days the ensuing season will make us a land of thistles, and scarce anything else.'

The Hobart Town Courier, December 1832.

Its origins lie in the Mediterranean basin and Asia Minor, but variegated thistle is now widespread. From Iceland to the South Island of New Zealand.

It's a serious weed. Of cultivation and disturbed habitats.

Once established it eliminates rivals, depriving them of sunshine, moisture and nutrients.

A seriously competitive weed.

Visitors to the island remarked on their abundance.

'*Thistles* are fast going ahead, all through Van Diemen's Land', wrote W. H. Harvey in 1855, echoing a journal entry made some twenty years previously by Charles von Hügel.

Newspaper editors and correspondents said that, if something wasn't done and done soon, a small problem would almost certainly become a large one.

'We have already said so much of these abominable

nuisances, that we almost despair of adding anything, except just to remind our country readers that prevention is better than cure.' Now was the time for people to start cutting, 'for if they do not kill the thistles, the thistles will starve them'.

Hobart Town Advertiser, January 1849.

They named names and pointed fingers.

'A small paddock, fronting the street leading to Lieutenant Simmons' villa...is now bearing a most luxuriant crop of thistles.'

Colonial Times, Hobart, February 1840.

'We were vexed to see, on Thursday last, a most flourishing crop of this noxious weed, – the seed just ripe for flitting – in front of the house, formerly occupied by Mr Roberts the soap-boiler, at the lower end of Macquarie street.'

The *Colonial Times* again, April 1840.

Almost everyone agreed there was a problem. But not everyone took the threat as seriously:

'We saw an article in the *True Colonist*, summoning to arms; and wondering what sudden invasion could have called forth such a warlike demonstration...we were induced to read on, in trembling anticipation lest the Aborigines had come down again in overwhelming numbers sufficient to annihilate our scattered forces, when we learned at last that the cry was against – *the thistles*.'

The Hobart Town Courier and Van Diemen's Land Gazette, July 1839.

The problem was thistles seemed to grow bigger and better in the southern hemisphere.

George P. Marsh cited the cardoon's breakout from

the gardens of Spanish colonies on the Plata. 'Vegetables, naturalized abroad either by accident or design, sometimes exhibit a greatly increased luxuriance of growth', he wrote in *The Earth as Modified by Human Action*.

W. P. Robertson again: 'When I left Scotland I thought I had left the country, par excellence, of thistles behind me. I now found that those of my native land, as compared with the "thistleries" of the Pampas, were as a few scattered Lilliputians to the serried ranks of the Brobdingnagians...In short, Pampa thistles, like all things else in South America, are on a large scale.'

How to explain this empire of thistles? These giants and their massive infestations? A medley of factors created particularly hospitable conditions, according to Alfred W. Crosby.

A Mediterranean climate similar to that of the plants' homeland.

Disturbances caused by land clearing for settlement and farming.

The impact of imported livestock on indigenous flora.

'Weeds thrive on radical change, not stability. That, in abstract is the reason for the triumph of European weeds in the Neo-Europes.'

Ecological Imperialism by Alfred W. Crosby, 1986.

Crosby's 'Neo-Europes' are regions settled by European emigrants and their descendants: North America, Australia, New Zealand and temperate parts of South America. The success of European imperialism in these countries, he argues, owed less to military and technological might and more to ecological serendipity.

In the library people arrive juggling laptops and folders.

Some settle in.

Some spread out.

Some go back and forth to the photocopiers, the stacks, the information desk.

Others leave for a seminar, a dinner date, one of those supersized US coffees.

It's dark when I leave and I stand for several minutes on the steps gazing at the moon in its sling of cloud. The stars. For city dwellers like myself, the night sky is our last frontier. More or less our sole experience of wilderness, and something that unites us with people across time and distance.

*

To view the past through the lens of the present is problematic, but images of *The Day of the Triffids* and other science fictions about aggressive plants taking over the world are hard to banish when I read the following:

The fecundity of thistles threatened the 'wool growing prosperity' of the colony, argued an unnamed settler in *The Observer* (Hobart) of March 1846. By way of illustration he presented a calculation to show how a mere eighty heads could reproduce to the tune of 7,962,624,000,000,000,000,000 'a progeny more than sufficient to stock not only the surface of the whole earth, but all the planets in the solar system'. He concluded with the cautionary example of Argentina: 'This is no vain supposition, for already, as you know, a species of thistle has destroyed the pasturage for hundreds of miles in South America.'

In *The War of the Worlds* by H. G. Wells, the Martians bring not only their weapons of destruction but also their plant species. And Martian red weed qualifies as a true alien invasive.

'Directly this extraordinary growth encountered water it straightway became gigantic and of unparalleled fecundity. Its seeds were simply poured down into the water of the Wey and Thames, and its swiftly growing and Titanic water fronds speedily choked both those rivers.'

'No cultivated plant has run wild on so enormous a scale as the cardoon (*Cynara cardunculus*) in La Plata', wrote Darwin in *The Variation of Animals and Plants under Domestication*.

Was it Darwin's thistles Wells had in mind when he created his red weed?

Probably.

A host of immigrant plants followed Europeans onto the savannahs of southern Africa, South America, Australia and New Zealand.

Some were deliberate imports. Others were stowaways competing for a place in the sun.

At the end of *David Copperfield*, when Charles Dickens sends a parcel of redundant characters to Australia, he describes their ship loaded for departure.

The 'bundles, and barrels, and heaps of miscellaneous baggage', the 'ploughman bodily carrying out soil of England on their boots'.

Some of these introduced species multiplied so quickly they changed the character of the landscape.

In 1913, W. J. Holland, director of the Carnegie Museums of Pittsburgh, labelled them the 'tramps of the vegetable world'.

Selected weeds of European and North American descent.

In the South Temperate Zone these adventitious species had found congenial ground, he wrote, 'and just as the people of Europe have exterminated the aborigines, so the weeds of Europe are exterminating the lowly plants of the region, and are surely taking possession of the soil'.

For England, Australia and the Americas beckoned not only as vast reservoirs of natural resources. They were also places to offload its 'surplus' population – primarily its poor and downtrodden. Way back in 1622, in *A Sermon Preached to the Honourable Company of the Virginian Plantation*, John Donne – otherwise one of my favourite poets – drew a bodily analogy. The purpose of the colony was like that of the spleen and liver whose role was 'to drain the ill humours' and 'breed good blood'.

That Darwin's theory of natural selection provoked outrage is well known. People raised their voices, shook their heads, waved their arms, jumped up and down. In other quarters his ideas were seized upon to provide dubious scientific and philosophical legitimacy.

For imperialist agendas.

For laissez-faire economics.

For the exploitation of the land.

Progress could now be understood as evolution. Onwards and upwards from primitive muddle to civilised order.

The Argentinian-born novelist and naturalist W. H. Hudson was introduced to the work of Darwin by his elder brother. Unlike the majority of English-speaking writers who passed through the Pampas, Hudson's knowledge of the region's flora was the product of prolonged proximity. His account of the 'thistle years' is vivid and oft quoted:

'Standing among the thistles in the growing season one could in a sense hear them growing, as the huge leaves freed themselves with a jerk from a cramped position, producing a cracking sound.'

Far Away and Long Ago, 1918.

The earth, wrote Michael and Edward Mulhall in their 1863 digest for prospective migrants, 'is covered with a rich carpet of clover and thistles, and looks as fine as any country with such a flat face can do'.

Flatness, monotony, nuisances posed by not-quite Europeans and thistles were features of the Pampas stressed by nineteenth-century authors, who cribbed and criss-crossed each other's narrative journeys.

Their thistle-portraits are generally alike in tone and content.

Occasionally, however, there are flashes of lyricism or idiosyncratic detail. Here are the Mulhall brothers again:

'About Christmas (midsummer) the thistles are all in full bloom, and soon droop and die…Pamperos, tremendous gales from the west, arise and sweep away all remains of vegetation. These hurricanes are so charged with dust and dead thistles that day becomes as dark as night.'

*

I'm browsing nineteenth-century tomes by men worried that the patterns they've imposed on the landscape are only skin-deep.

Many publications consist of disorganised correspondence, confusing chronologies and jottings with minimal editing or revision. None have an index. They have chapter summaries instead, which read like haphazard poetry. I'm tempted to compose my own:

Pampas giants – 'a most serious evil' – Darwin's mistake – new interruptions of thistles – counter-invasion strategies along legal lines – mishmash, hotchpotch, black sheep – what's missing? – the stories that lie beneath the thistle skirts – Mrs Miers.

Charles Mansfield, chemist and Christian Socialist, may have gone to South America to convalesce and philosophise, but most authors went for business. Wives went, too. Likewise daughters, nannies, governesses, female servants. But I've been unable to find any accounts by women. Not in English anyway. Although plenty of words were uttered on the subject of ladies' complexions and comportment, their lax morality and disregard for the conventions of polite society.

One or other of the Robertsons, J. P. or W. P. – I forgot to make a note of which – was shocked to see 'ladies, openly and undisguisedly, not only smoking, but smoking cigars of a size so large, that those of their male companions bore no comparison to them'.

Mrs Miers.

Mrs Miers was the wife of botanist and engineer John Miers. They married in 1818, the same year her husband was invited to join an expedition to develop copper mining in Chile. She was pregnant when they sailed from England. They anchored in Buenos Aires in 1819, where she fell ill with what was then called childbed fever.

Although Mrs Miers figures in *Travels in Chile and La Plata*, it's always as 'my wife'. I can find no mention of her first name – or indeed anything much about her. Online browsing yields the odd trace.

She was plucky. Several months pregnant, 'she *would* attempt the passage of the Cordillera…and it was a miracle that she and her infant did not perish in the mountains'.

The Monthly Review, 1826.

She had a second child. Maybe more.

No doubt she wrote – letters home, to friends, a favourite aunt.

Lists and household inventories.

Perhaps she kept a diary?

Translated her impressions into verse or vignettes...

How might she have written about the thistle forests that Darwin saw a decade later?

Botanical artist Marianne North was one of the few women who did publish travel memoirs.

Recognising thistles and other British flora in the vicinity of Deloraine when she visited Tasmania in 1881, she didn't mince her words: 'The country was not in the least attractive to me; it was far too English.'

*

It was 1882.

It was the Teatro Nacional in Buenos Aires.

Eduardo Holmberg gave a talk.

He was a biologist and writer of science fiction, and his talk aimed to illuminate the work of Darwin, who'd died that April.

Inside the theatre's auditorium, his audience shuffled in their seats, coughed, sighed, nodded, whispered, and occasionally let their minds wander.

To explain the struggle for existence Holmberg used a local example: a new or relatively new introduction he labelled black or devil's thistle (actually *Cirsium vulgare*) was successfully supplanting existing thistle species across the Pampas.

His scenario was significant because the outcome of this competition among thistles had consequences for the all-important cattle industry.

In the struggle for existence, thistles were stellar performers.

'Though flats may not be the precise characteristic of Van Diemen's Land, they can nearly rival the Pampas in the prolific production of Thistles.'

Hobart Town Advertiser, May 1848.

Although thistles thought to have come from California were identified as a problem in Tasmania in the 1830s, the colony's Californian Thistle Prevention Act wasn't proclaimed until 1870.

Under the terms of the Act, a Justice could require a landowner or tenant to remove thistles from their property. He could also authorise any person to enter land and search for thistles 'at any reasonable hour in the day-time'.

When The Californian Thistle Act 1878 replaced its predecessor, responsibility for enforcement was shifted to municipal inspectors. Any fines collected would be divided equally between the municipality and the person – whoever they were – who lodged the complaint.

Viewed from a distance the Pampas could almost be an expanse of meadow. Get closer and the scale – and sound – change. Above jagged grasses tower huge thistles, and the hum of mosquitoes and other insects is an ever-present acoustic backdrop.

On these treeless plains the variegated thistles were a source of fuel and a fall-back fodder in times of scarcity. On a less positive note, they provided a hideout for thieves and freebooters who would 'sally forth at night to rob and cut throats with impunity'.

But more than that.

In Argentina, Australia and elsewhere they created hybrid environments, neither indigenous nor exotic, but of tremendous vigour.

Another cloudless night outside the library.

I locate what may be the constellation Virgo, the only

female figure in the zodiac.

From points of light, whole mythologies unfurl.

But it's not only the stars; it's the space between them – the dark.

Plants, too, have a special place in folk and fairytales.

Forests.

Beanstalks.

Magic apples.

Instant hedges.

Why not thistles? Not all stories are about people, even if they involve them. Not all stories emphasise characters – in fact most fairytales do something quite different.

*

Botanists were on the lookout for any changes in the nature and behaviour of newcomers.

'It remains to be seen whether the altered circumstances of the acclimatised weeds, which seem to be so favourable to their growth, will prove permanent, or, by an over-stimulation, a change gradually effected in the constitution of the intruders, bringing about degeneracy and subsequent extinction.'

On the Naturalised Weeds and Other Plants in South Australia by Richard Schomburgk, 1879.

'The cardoon', wrote W. H. Hudson, 'is the European artichoke run wild and its character somewhat altered in a different soil and climate'.

The idea of reversion to the wild type was a commonly held belief.

Both Darwin and Joseph Hooker pointed out the lack of evidence for such a notion.

But the idea had staying power.

And resonance.

Resonance outside botany. Did transplanted Europeans

show the same tendency to run amok in the colonies of the south?

'A great deal of what we now term skylarking took place', wrote W. P. Robertson, 'romping and other freaks; till at last some of the most excited with wine proceeded to acts of indecorum, which, even in that latitudinarian country, could not be tolerated'.

Drinking.

Dancing.

Going native. Miers tells of an Englishman he met, an army deserter, who now with difficulty spoke his native tongue.

British stock hybridising with the locals.

Republicanism.

During *A Twelve Months' Tour in Brazil and the River Plate, with notes on sheep farming*, L. Dillon returned frequently to the topic:

'The Argentines to a man seem to be dreadfully republican in all their feelings and ideas. There is little distinction of classes in society. Every riff-raff cobbler, every rough *guacho* addresses you as *amigo* (Friend) in the most familiar manner, and sticks out his greasy paw to shake hands.'

'Australia, by a great many persons at home, is looked upon as a sort of moral waste-basket, in which to cast useless human scraps. And this, indeed, is the point we desire to emphasise, namely, that they are not a product of our own community, but only an accident in it. There is too much real life and genuine energy to permit of the Micawbers becoming indigenous. We get them as we get some kinds of refuse used for packing purposes.'

The Argus, Melbourne, February 1874.

Did rampant thistles play into anxieties within (and

without) colonial communities that they, too, might be the unwanted?

The upstarts. The outcasts.

The dregs.

The riff-raff of empire.

When he left New Zealand at the end of 1835, this was Darwin's parting shot: 'The greater part of the English are the very refuse of society.'

LAW

ILLEGAL THISTLES

I

In the beginning…was the law.

Deplorable condition was the verdict.

Thistles were the guilty party.

The quality of South Australian wool sent to London in 1842 was terrible. Flock owners were advised to keep their sheep out of pastures stocked with thistles and other bad seeds. Two years later, a subscriber to the *Adelaide Observer* drew attention to the large growth of thistles around town. These plants, he said, would be 'productive of great injury to all sorts of culture, if not eradicated'.

The 'abominable dissemination of thistles' had already been identified as a problem in Tasmania. The *Hobart Town Courier* of January 1836 predicted 'triumphant colonies [of the plants] in all parts of the island'.

It was a similar story in New South Wales.

And Victoria. If landholders remained indifferent to 'these vegetable plagues', bemoaned an 1849 *Geelong Advertiser* article, legislative interference would be necessary.

*

Midland Agricultural Association, Ross, 6 July 1848.

'Sir,——We beg leave to bring under his Excellency's notice the increasing growth of thistles…it is no exaggeration to say that many thousand acres are rendered entirely unprofitable, and unless some scheme can be devised to stop their progress, nothing appears more certain than that every acre in the colony will be overrun.'

James Bicheno, Colonial Secretary of Van Diemen's Land (and part-time scientist), replied. Although the Lieutenant-Governor was aware of the great and crying evil that was thistles, he believed the assent and co-operation of the mass of the community for stringent measures to curb them was lacking.

The Association wrote back – and upped the ante. They stressed 'the imperative necessity of introducing a legislative enactment to save the interests of this island, as a wool-growing and agricultural country, from ruin'.

This correspondence was tabled in the Legislative Council and a committee appointed 'to report upon the extent and best mode of meeting and remedying the evils accruing from the growth of thistles in this colony'. Said committee duly canvassed the opinions of the principal landholders and submitted its report in November 1848. While it recognised considerable diversity of sentiment about the form of any government intervention, it recommended not only legislative action but swift legislative action.

Which didn't happen.

It was over twenty years before The Californian Thistle Prevention Act of 1870.

*

The 'Cnicus arvensis' of the Tasmanian Act is Cirsium arvense, commonly known as creeping, perennial or Canadian thistle. It has a formidable root network, candelabras of mauve flowers and, despite the Canadian tag, it's a European original.

In a paper presented to the Royal Society of Tasmania in 1878, Francis Abbott traced the local name Californian thistle to a shipment of barley from California some twenty or twenty-five years previously. Although the plant itself 'has followed cultivation to most parts of the world, it is not improbable that it may have existed in the colony at a very early date'.

Whatever its migration history, *C. arvense*'s history as a weed is a long one. In 1640, in *The Theatre of Plants*, John Parkinson wrote: 'The Creeping way or Vineyard Thistle…as ill or worse than Quiche [probably couch grass] to weede out if it be once got into the ground.'

*

A year after its introduction, The Californian Thistle Prevention Act was amended to include a second species, *Cnicus lanceolatus*, since renamed *Cirsium vulgare*. We know it as the spear thistle; the 1871 amendment misnamed it as the Scotch thistle – as did the public and other parliaments, because at that time just about any purple-flowering thistle was dubbed Scotch.

A replacement act and amendments followed, but they applied only to the creeping (Californian) thistle. What happened to the spear thistle? The 1887 amendment stretched the word 'Thistle' to include the Bathurst burr. But still no spear thistle. It remained unregulated, outside the law, until The Local Government Act 1906 introduced the term 'noxious weed' and allowed the Governor of Tasmania to proclaim any plant as such.

II

The choir sings:

> We plough the fields and scatter
> The good seed on the land ——

I'm in Adelaide. City of churches and familiar tunes. That harvest hymn has German roots: it was *Wir pflügen und wir streuen* before it was an English standard.

Adelaide was the place I came to when I came to Australia.

I liked the cheesy jigsaw of the Covered Market. I liked the relative cool of the Botanic Garden and its Museum of Economic Botany, a wonderfully old-fashioned collection of glass cabinets and handwritten labels.

If I asked you to name an illegal plant, you'd probably say opium poppies or cannabis.

But in the beginning of South Australia...it was the thistle.

Emphatic as sunlight.

Unlike Tasmania, South Australia did move quickly on the matter of thistles.

28 December 1836 it was proclaimed a colony of the British Crown.

20 August 1851 the new Legislative Council met for the first time. A large crowd of spectators gathered at the entrance to the Supreme Court on Angas Street. Newspaper reports praised their respectability and restraint. Professional men, men of the church, regular citizens and 'a brilliant array of ladies'. The occasion 'was orderly in the extreme, as well became men endowed with free institutions...no fervour of display, no noise, save that of the artillery [a royal salute]'. What gravitas! What decorum!

October that same year William Giles, the elected member for Yatala, raised the problem of thistles at a meeting of the Central Road Board. Giles was a Protestant dissenter, something of a radical and something of a wowser who loathed the 'sins' of alcohol and theatre.

This is my heavily pruned version of that meeting:

Mr Giles would like to see a hundred men eradicating the thistles. It was not fully known how destructive they were.

The Chairman thought the question of thistles so important that the Board should express their opinions to the Governor or Council upon it.

Mr Giles thought the Government should introduce an Act.

Mr Randall thought the Act should be imperative on owners of lands to keep them clear of thistles.

Mr Giles would have an Act made to make them; there should be a penalty for not doing it.

Government accounts for 1850 show £33 8s spent on the cutting down and burning of thistles in Adelaide's Park Lands. Outside the city limits large areas that had been cleared for farming were covered with thistles. In Britain thistles grew in scattered patches and were a minor inconvenience. Here they were plants transformed. Tall and tight-packed, smothering the land all the way to the horizon.

Before he moved to Melbourne in 1852, Ferdinand von Mueller studied the florascape of South Australia. He estimated there were already some one hundred species which, 'having migrated, partly from Europe, partly from the Cape, have become naturalised here, beyond the possibility of extirpation'.

Prominent among that mob of weedy immigrants were… thistles.

A few days after the October meeting of the Central Road Board, thistles were debated by the Legislative Council. Along with judges' salaries, education and the appointment (or not) of a court interpreter for 'the inhabitants of this colony as are natives of Germany'.

Council members shared their personal experiences with thistles. One spoke about the plants using the lexis of medicine.

Mr Charles Hare said they might abate the evil even if they could not wholly cure it. A doctor was often employed to ease his patient, though he might not cure him.

And again:

The object was to get a grant of £500 to stay the disease, and then to bring in an act to cure it.

The land was thistle-sick.

I wonder if we think along preventive lines by framing the problem as an illness? And if we're pushed towards a punitive approach by adversarial language (e.g., fighting thistles).

Dragons and hippogriffs may have vanished from the map like extinct species, but the wild is still synonymous with danger. And when nature gnawed at the edges of nineteenth-century worldviews, they dramatised the encounters.

Of all the threats to the colony's peace and prosperity, chief among them it seems was...the thistle.

At the end of its first session the Legislative Council passed a batch of Acts governing pawnbrokers, the recovery of small debts, escapees from sister colonies, a life pension for (inland sea) explorer Charles Sturt...and thistles. An Act for preventing the further spread of the Scotch Thistle was passed on Friday 19 December 1851 and assented to on 2 January 1852. The first weed-control legislation in Australia, and possibly the world.

Pigs, cattle, rats, even insects were put on trial in medieval Europe. In Australia, thistles faced the might of the law.

Australia's most unwanted.

To early settlers Australia was geography without history. A place of environmental obstacles which had to be overcome or subdued to secure territorial and imaginative possession. Some ideas stick around, are hard to dispel, and that's one of them. Doesn't mean it's entirely true of course – one-size-fits-all ideas rarely are. Reality is more nuanced and complex and contradictory. No doubt some settlers were hoping to create an Englandshire Down Under, replete with rolling lawns and roses round the door, but many weren't. Yes, those undernourished, peely-wally immigrants were acutely aware of the society they'd left behind, but they were focused on the society they wished to build half a world away. They weren't so much looking to abandon Britishness as redefine it on their own, more idealistic, terms.

The names are solid Brit. A lot of Williams and Georges, the atmosphere congregational. Sure, there was paternalism and self-interest. The graziers who held sway in the legislature ensured the prompt carriage of the Thistle Act. Nevertheless, I'm impressed by the moral imagination of that first South Australian parliament.

Meanwhile, the thistles carried on – blasphemously purple, blasphemously fecund.

III

In the beginning God created the heaven and the earth, and on that earth He put thistles – to punish Adam and Eve for eating the forbidden fruit. To Eve He served a double punishment: not only painful childbirth but subordination to male authority. Sigh. To Adam God said: 'cursed is the ground for thy sake; in sorrow shalt thou eat of it all the days of thy life; Thorns also and thistles shall it bring forth to thee.'

Our Father who made the thistle
Who ruleth from kingdom above
Thy will be done where there is mayhem;
Give us this day our victory
Over those plants which trespass against us
Here and in places made strange by scripture;
Grant us this prayer, O Lord.

The Middle East is a very prickly place. It's always had an abundance of thorns, briars and thistles. A characteristic flora described in local accounts and in travelogues by visitors to the region. Writer, editor and philanthropist Emily Anne Beaufort mentioned dense crops of thistles in her 1861 book *Egyptian Sepulchres and Syrian Shrines*. As did other writers of the period, some of whom were trying to harmonise new scientific theories with Christian theology. (*The Origin of Species* was published in 1859.) One such figure was the Reverend Hugh Macmillan, a man of pious enthusiasm with a fair grasp of botany. *The Ministry of Nature* (1871) had a whole chapter devoted to thorns. Plants so armed, he said, represented a failure on the part of nature to reach perfection. He went on:

'Travellers call the Holy Land "a land of thorns." Giant thistles, growing to the height of a man on horseback, frequently spread over regions once rich and fruitful, as they do on the pampas of South America.' These plants, 'the evidences of a degenerate flora, and of deteriorated physical conditions, now form the most conspicuous vegetation of Palestine'.

For Macmillan nature was an open book alive with God's message, and ravenous weeds were pollutants whose control required man's eternal vigilance.

In *Purity and Danger*, anthropologist Mary Douglas identifies 'unclean' creatures as outliers within prevailing classification systems, those that exist between categories and/or inhabit multiple realms. That's the source of their danger. Thistles are plants of wilderness and grove, random and managed. Pests paradoxically valued for their medicinal properties; weeds useful as fodder and firewood; the Devil's creation, yet also culinary delicacies. In the western Mediterranean, wild thistles and thistle-doppelgängers, like *Gundelia tournefortii*, are stripped of their spines and cooked with meat or sautéed in olive oil.

In 2014 a Palestinian teenager and two friends in the West Bank were foraging for thistles – the kind used in local cooking. The boy was shot dead by the Israeli military, who claimed the trio were tampering with a security barrier. Flatbread has two sides, stories have more. However you read that incident, what matters is not the detail but the tragic, totally pointless death of a teenage boy.

Mary Douglas, who had a questing intellect, wrote about many things, including blame. In *Leviticus as Literature* she explored not only the scapegoat, but also the scapebirds that were used in the ritual cleansing of a leper.

Were thistles scapeplants?

IV

At some stage people stopped thinking of thistles as a Biblical curse and looked to the men of law, not the men of God, to deal with them. This positioned the plants not as divine retribution, but as offshoots of human activity.

Occasional advice from botanists appears in parliamentary records of the mid-nineteenth century, but the thistle problem was overwhelmingly regarded as a legal rather than scientific one.

Leichhardt.

Mueller.

Wilhelm Blandowski.

Richard Schomburgk.

Paweł Strzelecki.

Germans and Central Europeans were prominent in Australian science at that time, and indeed for much of that century.

By contrast, the law lay firmly within the British purview. Was that a factor in the decision to go the legal route?

*

Botany was one of the disciplines that emerged from eighteenth-century natural history. In the nineteenth it branched out as specialist fields developed. But the turn didn't take place until well into the twentieth century.

Botany gave way to plant science.

Researchers still study vegetal life but taxonomy and identification, once the cornerstones of botany, have been replaced by nucleotide sequences, biotech and data sets.

Along with haberdashery counters and fondue parties, the B-word has become an endangered entity.

V

'Like humans, imported noxious weeds thrive in Australia's sparkling air and under her hospitable conditions. They have come here by devious ways, and have developed friendly, tenacious habits...ingenious and resourceful, like their human kind again – they arrive hidden in the grass packing around breakable goods.'

The Advertiser, Adelaide, July 1932.

Thistles were insidious competitors at once familiar and foreign. They scared the settlers; as the plants spread, space for colonial enterprise decreased.

It starts with transported flora, with rapid acclimatisation, then suddenly the menace is all-pervasive and disaster just a hop, skip and a hayseed away. The cry goes up:

Something must be done!

*

'The plant is again running rapidly up to flower, and a few more hot days will arm every wind that blows with the floating plague.'

The Argus, Melbourne, November 1850.

Victoria, too, opted for legislative action, and in 1856 passed An Act to make provision for the eradication of certain Thistle Plants and the Bathurst Burr.

Fruitfulness would come not only from God above and the earth below, but from faith in the rule of law, and this particular law required owners and lessees to destroy any of the four named thistles growing on their property. Thistle inspectors were appointed; landholders and tenants who didn't comply were prosecuted. Yet thistles had their advocates and the passage and policing of this Act, its successors and subsequent amendments, generated considerable, sometimes passionate, debate in government circles, in clubs and country towns, and of course in the press.

Community concerns were expressed through flurries of correspondence in the pages of Melbourne and regional newspapers. Many insisted the scale of the nuisance had been seriously underestimated.

The *Portland Guardian* of December 1858 complained that thistles were 'enjoying a carte blanche' around the Wannon River in southwest Victoria. 'We had the wars of the roses, and why not the wars of the thistles?'

'Observant men in the pastoral districts have long recognised the cultural powers of the thistle; how by the growth and subsequent decay of its roots it opens up the soil, admitting air and moisture to considerable depths, and thus preparing it for sustaining vegetation of a superior order.'
The Australasian, May 1871.

Arguments about thistles' value in tillage or as contingency fodder for times of drought leaked into broader questions of responsibility and fairness.

'It is over-legislation. It is unjust. It is oppressive...[thistles are] not a legitimate subject for legislation', wrote cattle farmer Charles Macknight in an argumentative letter to *The Australasian*.

The *Geelong Advertiser* sat on the fence:
No one could dispute the tremendous spread of thistles, but 'the question which still demands solution is whether their power for evil or for good is the greater, and on that point the evidence is still most conflicting. It is impossible to overlook the damage to the wool where thistles have become even moderately thick.'

Always wool.
The history of thistles is woven
into the history of wool.

Victoria's 1856 Act covered four thistle species: variegated, spear, Scotch and one known as the blessed, holy or sacred thistle.

Fact check: Although the Act named it *Carduus Benedictus*, the blessed thistle's official botanical name has been updated to *Cnicus benedictus*.

The inclusion of the blessed thistle is surprising. Was it a mistake? The first herbarium record of the plant in Australia is 1904. It seems to occur only sporadically in a few parts of the southeast and, as far as I can tell, has never been a problem. If anything, the reverse: *Cnicus benedictus* is recognised as a herbal remedy and has been for centuries.

This is from the 1809 reprinting of Culpeper's 1652 tome *The English Physician*: 'It is called Carduus Benedictus, or Blessed Thistle, or Holy Thistle: I suppose the name was put upon it by some that had little holiness in themselves...It helps swimmings and giddiness of the head, or the disease called Vertigo...strengthens the attractive faculty in man... drinking the decoction of it helps red faces, tetters and ring-worms...plague, sores, boils, and itch, the bitings of mad dogs and venomous beasts.'

It's also one of Shakespeare's thistles. In *Much Ado about Nothing* Margaret recommends it as a treatment to Beatrice. (Back then a qualm was not only a misgiving, but also a medical symptom.)

'Margaret: Get you some of this distilled Carduus Benedictus, and lay it to your heart: it is the only thing for a qualm.

Hero: There thou prick'st her with a thistle.

Beatrice: Benedictus! why Benedictus? you have some moral in this Benedictus.

Margaret: Moral! no, by my troth, I have no moral meaning; I meant, plain holy-thistle.'

I wonder how the Legislative Council decided which thistles to prohibit? Their choice verges on the arbitrary and parliamentary transcripts provide few clues. Victoria's Government Botanist, Ferdinand von Mueller, was expeditioning in northern Australia from mid-1855 and unavailable to advise. Was the input of other botanists sought? My search finds no evidence. If other botanists were consulted it was informally, perhaps over port and cigars in a gentleman's club? At the cricket? Or during interval at the just opened Theatre Royal?

Victoria in the 1850s was a lively place. Melbourne was one of the world's busiest wool ports – wool again – and the gold rushes were bringing prosperity and population to the colony. Along with a growing demand for entertainment.

Act two ends on a cliffhanger. The curtain comes down and the audience leave their seats for an intermission drink or bite of supper. Perhaps an honourable member and a senior botanist talk thistles in the upper circle...

Imagination animates the past, multiplying its possibilities like a house with countless rooms; sometimes it's the only way to engage with what might have happened.

The same four species remained when the 1856 Act was repealed and replaced by The Thistle Prevention Statute 1865.

Several years later changes to the Act were again contemplated and this time Mueller was consulted. In an 1871 communication to the President of the Board of Land

and Works and Premier, he recommended the removal of the blessed thistle from the banned list. It had 'lately almost disappeared, it moreover having never been really abundant'. He also recommended the addition of the creeping thistle and the marsh thistle. None of his suggestions were taken up.

Mueller wasn't universally popular; his position as Director of the Melbourne Botanic Garden was under review and he was frequently attacked in the press and from the floor of parliament. Was that why his advice was ignored? Or was it something more pedestrian like paperwork mislaid or wrongly filed?

What really puzzles me, though, is Mueller's inclusion of the plant he called *Carduus palustris* (now *Cirsium palustre*), the marsh thistle or European swamp thistle. As its name indicates, it likes damp settings. In Canada, the northern United States and New Zealand it grows in high-rainfall areas.

It has never been found in Australia.

Although it did appear here in print. As *Cnicus palustris* in J. D. Hooker's *On the Flora of Australia* and in Bentham's *Flora Australiensis*. Both placed it in Tasmania.

The most likely scenario is that it was misidentified by both Hooker and Mueller. In his 1871 communication, the Government Botanist wrote that the marsh thistle and the creeping thistle had 'invaded more lately this colony, probably from Tasmania, were they are long naturalised, and I deem it particularly desirable that these should be included [in the Act] as both are troublesome'.

Yes, creeping thistle was a worry, but I wonder what plant it was that Mueller mistook for the marsh thistle.

July 1875 revisions to The Thistle Prevention Stature were being debated in the Legislative Assembly and the question of which species to include arose.

'Mr Bosisto: The most advisable plan would be to insert the botanical and vernacular names of all the objectionable thistles growing in this colony, for the purpose of identification.

Mr Macpherson: It would be well to make the interpretation of the word thistle as broad as possible, and simply exclude the sow thistle, which was a very useful weed.

After some discussion ——

Mr Godfrey: There had always been a great difficulty in defining what a thistle was; and if the amendment was carried, any person growing an artichoke would be liable to be fined, for that was a thistle ——

Mr Macpherson: It is not commonly known as a thistle.

Mr Godfrey: Ah, but a clever lawyer might prove that it was.'

Mistaken identity is a recurring theme.

Who are we when we're not who we think we are?

The 1885 amendment added creeping thistle.

But the blessed thistle remained. One of the six species named in the Thistle Act 1890.

With the amendment at the end of 1891 the reach of the Act – and the linguistic reach of the word 'thistle' – was greatly expanded by the Governor in Council having authority to declare any plant to be a thistle. Initially an extra four thistles (shore, star, saffron and Malta) were added, but over the following years furze, blackberry, St John's wort and a host of other plants all became 'thistles'.

By 1909 there were forty-two plants, including five native species, pronounced 'thistles' under the Act, 'on account of their obnoxious or poisonous character and rapid powers of multiplication'.

The Weeds, Poison Plants, and Naturalized Aliens of Victoria by Alfred J. Ewart and J. R. Tovey.

The Thistle Act 1915 named the five species specifically identified in previous acts, plus 'any plant named and declared to be a thistle in any proclamation'. Thistle became a collective noun, a bucket, a catch-all term not only for true thistles and thistle-like plants, but for any plant judged undesirable.

VI

Anti-thistle laws weren't unique to Australia.

The US state of Connecticut passed a law in 1821 prohibiting the sale of forage crop seeds that contained seeds of Canada (i.e., creeping) thistle. Similar legislation was enacted in other states and in 1872 Illinois passed An Act concerning Canada thistles.

There was The Canada Thistle Act of Upper Canada 1865.

The co-starring species of North American thistle laws were the creeping and Russian thistles.

Edwin R. Spencer called the former a 'rogue of rogues among weeds'. Creeping thistle had, he claimed in *All About Weeds* (1940), not 'a single virtue so far as man is concerned'.

New Zealand's anti-thistle ordinances took a broader brush to the problem. In February 1854 Wellington passed An Act to prevent the propagation of certain plants known as Thistles. Other provinces (as they were then called) followed with their own wordings and specifics.

The line between the natural world and politics is porous. The concept of nature is malleable, and our relationship with plant life has always been deeply political. Especially in settler societies like Australia.

But not only in settler societies.

Imagine a town a short drive from the Belgian–Dutch border. Imagine a resident going about her usual business – perhaps she's a music teacher or a paramedic. Out of the blue, she receives an official letter telling her she will be fined unless she removes a thistle that's growing in her garden. You don't imagine that happening in 2015, but it did.

Under an 1887 law still in operation, Belgians are required to remove thistles from field and yard. The original aim of the legislation was to protect farmers who risked contracting tetanus if they scratched themselves on a thistle and then came into contact with horse dung.

The thistle is the opposite of the missing explorer or the lost child that 'disappeared into the bush never to be found' narrative that haunts the psyche of white Australia. Thistles don't vanish despite the various acts designed to make them go away.

Our fears stare back at us from the thickets of the mind.

In Britain they were unremarkable plants but in Australia, New Zealand and the Americas the lusty thistle acquired a new identity and increased significance.

If the Dutch had tulip mania in the seventeenth century, Australia had thistle panic in the nineteenth.

VII

Documents from the Swiss city of Lausanne record the prosecution of an eel.

In France a bevy of rats was tried in ecclesiastical court for the wanton destruction of the barley harvest. (They allegedly ate the crop.)

Germany 1499, a bear was in the dock accused of murder.

In *The Criminal Prosecution and Capital Punishment of Animals,* E. P. Evans chronicles the animal trials that took place, mainly in Europe, mainly in the Middle Ages. Caterpillars, weevils, worms, moles, mules, dogs, dolphins – a Noah's ark of creatures were charged with crimes of property damage and human injury. The reasoning behind many of these cases was that the devil might be controlling those who weren't strictly Christian. This made vulnerable Moors, Jews, unmarried women, assorted non-conformists and non-human animals.

Did plants have their days in court? A yew accused of poisoning someone with its berries, for example. Or beetroots that failed to reproduce.

My research draws a blank, but ——

There is the fruitless fig tree of the New Testament which, when cursed by Jesus, immediately withered. 'Every tree that bringeth not forth good fruit is hewn down, and cast into the fire.' You can take this sentence at face value: a horticultural tip about getting rid of a cumberer of the orchard. Alternatively, you can interpret it as punishing the tree for its delinquency.

If I were a lawyer defending the fig tree, this is what I'd argue:

To institute judicial proceedings against a thistle, or any plant, first you need to endow it with sentience or some kind of moral barometer. How else can you prove that it's conscious of its misdeed?

Towards the end of my undergraduate degree and before I hit on postgrad study as my next stage, I toyed with the idea of a career in law. My mother once told me that for ages she expected me to become a barrister because I liked arguing so much.

'You were born breech,' she reminded me. Feet first. A portent of the headstrong and difficult person you've grown up to be.

I was interested in jurisprudence, in the philosophical underpinnings of the legal system. But it seemed there was a lot of conveyancing or defending drunk drivers before you got to ethical dilemmas and big-picture questions of justice. Although I eschewed law as a profession, I've delved into some of those big-picture issues in my playwriting. Legal principles aren't neutral or universal; they emerge from and are answerable to particular traditions and interests. My play *Songket* asks: what happens when one person's culture is another's crime?

In the penultimate act of *The Merchant of Venice* when Gratiano attacks Shylock, he refers to a wolf 'hanged for human slaughter'. This may be a reference to one of those animal trials. Or to the practice of usury. Elizabethans denounced usurers as heretics and wolves. In contemporary usage, we've swapped the wolf for another creature: the loan shark.

Although classified as one of Shakespeare's comedies, I look at *The Merchant of Venice* as a revenge tragedy wedged into a romantic comedy. The play's anti-Semitism has been much discussed, but it's also the quintessential legal drama with a female advocate in a leading role – albeit disguised as a man.

After 'the quality of mercy is not strained, it droppeth as

the gentle rain from heaven', Portia finds a loophole in the agreement between Antonio and Shylock and exploits it to win the case.

No wonder courtroom scenes feature in so many films, TV series and plays. Courtrooms are inherently theatrical. The costumes, the splash and thrash of words, the juxtaposition of reason and emotion.

When it comes to legal drama, here are my top five plays:

The Crucible. Arthur Miller's retelling of the Salem witch trials.

Two. *Witness for the Prosecution*. I've included this for sentimental reasons. Agatha Christie's play is a creaky old thing, sexist and xenophobic. I saw an amateur production of it in a draughty church hall when I was about twelve or thirteen. When one of the actors broke character and refused to continue until people in the audience stopped whispering, it opened my eyes to the possibilities of live performance.

Three. *The Winslow Boy*. Terence Rattigan's play also shows its age. But its exploration of establishment clout and the pursuit of justice whatever the cost makes for compelling drama.

Four. *Chicago*, the 1926 play by Maurine Dallas Watkins that inspired the film and musical adaptations. A wild Jazz Age satire about murder and media manipulation, it drew on real-life trials (as did *The Winslow Boy*) that Watkins covered as a reporter for the *Chicago Tribune*.

And *Les Plaideurs* (*The Litigants*) by seventeenth-century French playwright Jean Racine. A crazy burlesque of compulsive litigants, judicial prolixity and a dog on trial for stealing a chicken from His Honour's kitchen.

VIII

On the subject of thistle acts, the different colonies had similar concerns:

Expense.

Enforcement.

Encroachment on the rights of individuals.

Once there was consensus about the need to get rid of thistles, the next question was: who would do the heavy lifting?

'We believe, there are several worn-out men, about the Prisoners' Barracks, who would be able to attend to this light but important employment.'

Colonial Times, Hobart, October 1839.

If not prisoners, perhaps the poor?

'We might venture to suggest that applicants for Government relief might be profitably employed in eradicating those pests before they spread their species in every direction.'

The Adelaide Observer, November 1848.

Or women, the elderly, even children?

June 1852

To the Editor of the *Adelaide Observer.*

'Sir——It is evident from its present state what must be the consequences to the Colony, if this insidious but gigantic enemy is not resolutely attacked with a view to its complete extermination...

'The weed of this year's growth can yet be easily destroyed by women and children, or men who, from age, are unfitted for more laborious occupation...and such persons would not require more than a very moderate rate of pay.'

'Children would do it very well; even a boy of nine years old would do as well as a man.'

Robert Massie Esq., witness examined by the Select Committee on the Scotch Thistle and Bathurst Burr, New South Wales, 1852.

It was frequently suggested that clearing the baneful weed was a job for Aboriginal people.

'A couple of parties of twenty blacks each, with an energetic white overseer, would do wonders. Let them be furnished with clothing for the lower man of sufficient strength to turn the short spikes of the hoe; let them be supplied, *while if they work*, with ample rations, and a little tobacco.'

The Argus, Melbourne, November 1850.

And Aboriginal children.

'Thistles on the Park Lands are now from one to two inches above ground. Government incurred a considerable expense last year in cutting them down after they had reached maturity. It would be very easy to cut them down now, and it would be good exercise for the Native School children to keep them down.'

The Adelaide Times, March 1851.

Failing that, why not workers imported for the task from China or India? The 1852 New South Wales Select Committee on the Scotch Thistle and Bathurst Burr received a number of proposals along these lines.

From the Bench of Magistrates, Wollombi.

'We would suggest that the Legislature should place at the disposal of the Executive, the means of obtaining and employing, for a limited period, a numerous body of Asiatics, from the Territories of the East India Company.'

From Charles Campbell Esq.

'Three or more Chinamen might be placed at the disposal of each Country Bench of Magistrates, to be employed for twelve months in rooting up the weeds in question.'

Who would do the heavy lifting?

The incarcerated, the indigent, the infirm, the indentured and the Indigenous.

IX

Irish folklore tells of poets reciting verse to protect fields of wheat and grain from vermin, of rhyming the rats to death.

Shakespeare refers to it in *As You Like It* when Rosalind, deluged with poems from her would-be lover, says:

'I was never so be-rhymed since

Pythagoras' time, that I was an Irish rat, which I

can hardly remember.'

Transpose that practice to Australia and let's see if we can rhyme away the thistles.

Reverse the curse of Genesis.

*

Queensland's thorny problem was the prickly pear.

Western Australia had The Spanish Radish and Scotch Thistle Prevention Act 1874.

New South Wales tried several times to bring in legislation to control the spread of thistles. Here's a chronology:

1852. The Scotch Thistle Bill was introduced in the Legislative Council. During its second reading George Macleay said that he had personally seen thistles six feet tall growing over vast tracts of the interior. He reminded the House that they held the lands of the colony not for themselves alone, but for those who might come after them. A Select Committee was appointed 'to Inquire into the facts connected with the introduction of the Scotch Thistle and Bathurst Burr into this Colony; the progress these weeds have made in the different Districts; the present evil accruing to the Colony from their existence; and what means (if any), should be had recourse to for their extirpation'.

Six months later the Committee reported back.

Thistles were a serious problem; at some point in the future legislation to stay the progress of the evil would be necessary. But because of the labour shortage 'at the present moment, it is not expedient to legislate upon the subject'. They recommended reappointing a Committee in the next Session of the Council.

And there the Bill stopped.

April 1865 Sir William Manning introduced The Bathurst Burr, Dock, and Thistle Bill. A fortnight later he withdrew it. It would cost thousands of pounds and ruin many to compel them to destroy those plants.

Four years later there was another attempt: The Cumberland and Camden Bathurst-Burr and Thistle Bill. Another Select Committee was appointed.

Arguments flipped hither and yon and went round in circles. How *do* you stop thistles growing, ripening and broadcasting their seed?

'To the Members of the Legislative Assembly.

Gentlemen,

On an estate such as the one I occupy there are deep gullies and rocky ravines into which it would be difficult for a man to crawl, but, where, nevertheless, the thistle finds its way. It would be exceedingly difficult in such a case to wholly eradicate it... This bill renders the owner or occupier liable to be fined £20 every *thirty* days, on the information of '*any person*' who, by diligent search, might espy a thistle growing, even if it should be growing in the most inaccessible place...

Yours &c.,

Clements Lester.'

3 November 1869.

The Bill had a second reading, and in November 1870 a

third. It was then passed to the Upper House.

February 1871 the House went into Committee to consider the Bill in detail. After debating the slipperiness of thistle names the discussion moved on:

Sir T. A. Murray could find no precedent in the parliamentary records of the mother country for legislation of this kind.

Mr Darley also stated his inability to find any precedent for this Bill in British legislation. He thought it ought to be postponed.

Sir William Macarthur said a wide distinction should be made between the circumstances of a new country and an old one. On lands after long occupation those noxious plants seemed to have far less power of reproduction than when first introduced.

The debate dawdled on.

Some thought the extirpation of thistles a lost cause.

Others held firm to their belief:

The law could overcome nature.

The geometry of their arguments was pragmatic with none of the wonkspeak and spin that's engulfed so much of today's public discourse.

There was friction.

There was ego.

There was brouhaha and fiery rhetoric. But rhetoric isn't reality. And The Cumberland and Camden Bathurst-Burr and Thistle Bill was abandoned at the end of April 1871.

With The Local Government Act 1906 (and the approval of the Governor) councils finally acquired the means to declare a plant noxious.

X

The thistles grew on regardless.

'Like wickedness in a city's slums', according to Francis Myers (pen name Telemachus) writing about the Riverina in 1890.

'We approach another crop miles broad and very high… It stretches away as far as we can see, and when we come at it it is of thistles. Long, lank, wicked prickled thistles. Not stiff and sturdy like Scotch-men, nor luscious like the spotted-leaved things to which tradition ascribes so strange and sacred an origin, but bad things altogether.'

Did those various acts arrest the spread of thistles?

In a word: no.

The failure of early legislation can be attributed to a number of factors.

First up, thistles don't recognise human laws.

Secondly, although there were prosecutions, farmers and landlords refused to abide by laws they deemed unfair, and remained unbowed by the coercive muscle of government.

Victoria had an army of civil servants whose duty was to inspect holdings and report negligent owners, but elsewhere the policing of thistles was piecemeal and usually left to local bodies.

Behold the thistle.

'In a court of law it is not necessary to examine what one might call the moral character of the weed. The prosecution merely produces a gazette proclamation and the weed therein referred to is a noxious weed. The Gazette is its final condemnation. Noxious weeds, unlike poets, are made – not born.'

The Sydney Morning Herald, February 1934.

*

Aboriginal nations, Afghan cameleers, the yellow peril, postwar refugees, asylum seekers sent to offshore detention centres. Australia's villains change shape. Scapegoats and pariahs may eventually be redeemed – well, some of them. But Anglo-Celtic Australia is always the storyteller, for ever and ever plying a narrative with itself as the protagonist, the underdog hero courageously defending its borders, its history, its lifestyle, its so-called Christian values from whoever or whatever has been cast as the latest threat.

*

This morning Adelaide is hot, awash in dusty yellow air. One of those days you can practically touch the weather. I'm strolling along North Terrace, past Old Parliament House, built in 1855 to replace the single chamber where that first Legislative Council met and debated thistles. Past the current parliament building.

Around Government House, the wall goes up. I imagine the original inhabitants, counted as lesser beings, fodder for evangelists, chased from their land.

The choir sings:

We plough the fields and scatter

The good seed on the land ——

Decades of civic life have settled comfortably on North Terrace. Buildings of stone rise from the ground. But instead of the important men commemorated in granite and bronze I'm thinking about the shipwrights and cooks, the barmaids and bell-hangers, the notaries, ironmongers, forwarding agents, tea merchants and straw-hat makers. And the goods and chattels and seedlife they brought with them.

To those migrants from the cold and fog of northern Europe, the heat in summer was brutal. Streets were unsurfaced. Dirt stirred by cartwheels caught in their throats. Down their backs, inside their wrong-climate clothes, streamed salty Niagaras of sweat.

The choir sings:
We plough the fields and scatter
The good seed on the land ——

In the beginning...was the thistle.

MUELLER'S THISTLE PAMPHLET

Dr Ferdinand von Mueller steps into the witness box. Swears by Almighty God and gives his evidence in German-accented English. The town is Bacchus Marsh, some sixty kilometres from Melbourne. Once a stopover on the way to the Ballarat goldfields, now a thriving agricultural centre. The two-storey sandstone building on Main Street is, this Tuesday 17 February 1874, home to the Court of Petty Sessions, the lowest tier of the judicial system which attends to minor crimes and matters under £20. Outside, the weather is unsettled. Inside, the cedarwood fittings have been polished to a warm glow.

The Bench: a Police Magistrate and two justices of the peace.

The case: Thistle Inspector Kissock versus William Johnston.

The charge: neglecting to cut thistles.

Defendant says he has used endeavours to eradicate the thistles growing on his property. But it is impossible to get rid of them all.

Dr Mueller confirms he is the Government Botanist. And that the plant specimen shown him is *Carduus lanceolatus*. Popular name: spear thistle.

Mr Kissock asks if *C. lanceolatus* is the emblem of the Stuarts.

The Bench deems that question immaterial.

Dr Mueller is then questioned about the germinating properties of the seeds. And the proper time for removing thistles. He says the best time is when the thistles are running into flower. Not when they are actually in flower, because by that stage the seeds would have perfected their growth in the floweret.

Mr Kissock verifies that he served the appropriate notice. In response to a question from the Bench, he states that when he served the defendant he found twenty or thirty acres uncut.

Mr Johnston requests more time.

His Worship asks if he has any evidence that he used endeavours to eradicate the thistles.

After some deliberation the Bench fixes the fine at £5.

Dr Mueller declines a fee.

Next case. Same offence.

Harbingers of high summer, thistles are dramatic.

To the good burghers of Bacchus Marsh and other rural townships they're a pest.

Thistles were never swing[1], never behind the scenes, also-ran weeds. In the nineteenth century they were centre-stage.

Terrorists of the plant world.

Thistles were of such concern to the Victorian Department of Agriculture that in July 1893 – somewhat late in the piece, given the first Thistle Act was passed in 1856 – they published a pamphlet entitled *Illustrated Description of Thistles, Etc., Included Within the Provisions of the Thistle Act of 1890* written by Ferdinand von Mueller.

*

---

1 Swing is a musical theatre term for ensemble members who understudy several roles.

A twice-naturalised German immigrant, Ferdinand Müller arrived in Australia in 1847, removed the umlaut from his surname – a gesture symbolic as well as pragmatic – and began work at Büttner & Heuzenroeder Chemists in Adelaide. Five years later, at the age of twenty-seven, he was appointed Victoria's Government Botanist, a newly created position that he held until his death in 1896.

A prolific author of books, monographs, scientific papers, leaflets and compendia, he maintained a deep commitment to public education. Mueller wanted people to learn about plants not only because they were interesting in and of themselves, but also to understand their economic worth. To this end, he provided expert advice, operated a plant identification service for communities in regional Victoria (and further afield), gave lectures, and wrote practical guides like *Illustrated Thistles*.

*

I'm always struck by the theatricality of nineteenth-century science. Geology, botany, zoology and other disciplines were popularised and publicised in performative forms. Speeches, son et lumière, dioramas, dialogues.

The idea of communicating information by way of dialogue harks back to Plato. Later contributors to this genre I think of as non-fiction drama for the page include Galileo, Fontenelle – and Jane Marcet, whose *Conversations* take place between Mrs B, a fictional tutor, and her pupils, Caroline and Emily. *Conversations on Vegetable Physiology* (1829) consists solely of dialogue organised into segments or scenes. And although there are no stage directions, the setting is easily imagined from the characters' interactions.

*

In a talk given at the Ballarat Farmers' Club in 1873, the Reverend Mr Potter said that he 'hoped the learned professions would aid the farmers by bringing science to bear upon the culture of the soil'. It was a sentiment echoed across the colony. Yet botanists, transfixed by the novelty and strangeness of Australian native flora, were disinclined to study introduced weeds.

On the whole.

Mueller wrote *Illustrated Thistles* at the behest of the Secretary for Agriculture. It was distributed gratis to councils, schools, libraries, agricultural societies, individual graziers and other interested parties. It was a tangible response to the myriad requests for 'information respecting various Thistles which have taken root in the colony of Victoria'.

The pamphlet describes in detail eight thistle species plus the Bathurst burr. Mueller uses their Latin appellations. Here are their common names:

Spear thistle.

Creeping thistle.

The shore or slender thistle.

Variegated thistle.

The Scotch (heraldic) thistle.

Star thistle.

Malta thistle and

Saffron thistle.

'This unpretensive publication arose from a desire of facilitating an exact knowledge of those plants', wrote Mueller in his introduction. 'In the winterless clime of our lowlands the growth of weeds proceeds more or less through the whole year and this renders coping with such plants here far more onerous than in countries where the length and severity of the winters annihilate largely such plants and their seeds.'

Given that most landholders and administrators regarded *all* thistles as weeds to be eliminated, why did they need to recognise the different species? I've not found any correspondence about the commissioning of *Illustrated Thistles* but, patchworking from other sources, it's clear that identifying the specific species proclaimed under the Act had become a legal and political quagmire.

Distinguishing one kind of thistle from another is tricky – even for experienced botanists. A Noxious Plants Conference held in Canberra in 1985 ran a Thistle Identification Competition for delegates. Out of seventy entrants, only two were able to identify the rosettes of all sixteen species.

Concerns along these lines had been expressed from the outset. 'Farmers are not botanists, and many, like myself, not troubled with too much brains', declared one correspondent in a long, indignant letter to the editor of *The Argus* in 1856.

In 1871 the same newspaper reported that during a meeting of municipal representatives in Melbourne a participant stumbled over the string of Latin terms. Thistles should be named in plain English, he grumbled, because few persons in the country could understand their 'chemical names'.

From shire authorities' point of view, disputes about identification and how to interpret the word 'thistle' were making it hard to obtain and sustain convictions. How it could go wrong is demonstrated by the case of G. Oliver, Thistle Inspector, versus the Hutton Brothers. In March 1870 the justices at Penshurst Court of Petty Sessions fined Messrs W. and J. Hutton £100 for permitting thistles to grow in five paddocks. The Thistle Inspector had shown the court a specimen he'd found on the defendants' land. A Dr Dickenson had identified the plant and confirmed that it was one of the proscribed thistles.

An appeal against this judgment was made to Judge Cope at the Court of General Sessions in Hamilton:

Mr Pridham appears for the appellants. Only five species of thistle are tabooed by the statute. There are hundreds of varieties it is perfectly legal to grow. Yes, the thistle is a nuisance. But that being so, it is essential to designate the *particular* form of nuisance – just as one would cite a bone-mill or slaughterhouse, or indeed any other annoyance. To be rendered tenable, the conviction must state that the plants growing on the Hutton property are one of the five prohibited species.

Mr Duigan, on behalf of the respondents, counters. He interprets the Act differently. To allow any kind of thistle to grow on your land is to bring oneself within the pale of the law.

Judge Cope upholds the appeal. The conviction must state, and prove, that the thistles in question are one or other of the following: *Carduus lanceolatus, Carduus marianus, Carduus Benedictus, Onopordum acanthium* or *Xanthium spinosum*.

One less ambiguity in a case that was nothing but.

The press and others were quick to point out the implications.

'With this decision we may expect that at every charge preferred against the thistle growers we shall have an array of scientific men to prove that the thistles in question do or do not belong to one of the five kinds.'

The Kyneton Guardian, Victoria, June 1870.

Disputes along these lines continued. In courts across Victoria the actors changed but the basic drama did not. It played on a circuit like a touring show.

Beneath blue forever skies

Thistles bounced gently on their stems.

There were repeated calls to address the problem of identification 'by requesting the Government Botanist to prepare a supplement…containing coloured figures and diagrams' of the banned plants. Shire councils were reluctant to pay expert witnesses to travel from Melbourne, and it was unreasonable to expect thistle inspectors to 'read themselves up in the subject sufficiently to give them status as experts. The only thing that can be done is to possess each thistle inspector and each clerk of petty sessions with such pictorial evidence as we have pointed out and then, possibly, conviction may be procured.'

The Ballarat Star, October 1871.

Hence *Illustrated Description of Thistles, Etc., Included Within the Provisions of the Thistle Act of 1890*. A publication designed to help those on the land identify the verboten thistles.

*

Did the booklet serve its expected purpose? How was it received? Beyond the occasional footnote, *Illustrated Thistles* rates barely a mention in the various biographies, collected correspondence and articles about Mueller and his legacy. It's difficult to find evidence of the extent to which the handbook was used by its intended constituency, but my sense is not much.

At their April 1893 meeting, the Government Botanist gave members of the Field Naturalists' Club of Victoria a preview. They were shown proof plates of thistles which had been drawn by Mr P. Ashley under Mueller's direction.

More on those later.

The Gippsland Times called it very instructive and

The Queenslander claimed that 'any ordinary observer with the aid of this pamphlet will be able to determine the names of all thistles growing on his land'. That same month, July 1893, an article in *The Leader* explained the reasoning behind *Illustrated Thistles*:

'The idea of bringing out this publication is owing to a desire to facilitate the acquirement of a knowledge of those objectionable plants on the part of landowners...clear descriptions of the thistles and thistle like plants mentioned in the act are provided, so that the various species can be easily identified.'

Reactions from colleagues were – let's say, spare. In October 1893 Eugene W. Hilgard, a professor of agricultural chemistry in California, wrote: 'Your paper on thistles has also greatly interested me, since the weed question is with us also an alarming one.'

Fellow botanist J. H. Maiden referenced *Illustrated Thistles* in articles and books. As did Freda Detmers in her bulletin *Canada Thistle*, published in the United States by the Ohio Agricultural Experiment Station in 1927.

Those were the polite responses.

Although Mueller wrote that 'it is desirable that the naming of the Thistles here hitherto immigrated and copiously spread should be as free from complication as possible', his *Illustrated Thistles* is not, by any standard, an easy read. November 1893 *The Alexandra and Yea Standard* pointed this out by quoting at length his description of the Scotch thistle, prefacing their excerpt with the comment, 'if the farmer can make much of it he is cleverer than we are'.

Here's a sample of Mueller's text:

'Stamens alternate to the corolla-lobes, their filaments almost glabrous; anthers connate, linear-sagittate, purplish. Style capillulary; stigmas narrowly semicylindric, coherent, except at the summit, with a slight basal enlargement.' And so on through all nine species. No wonder he wrote in the introduction that his description 'may seem unnecessarily effuse'.

As clear as mud. Twelve months later, another newspaper from regional Victoria, *The Kyabram Union and Rodney Shire Advocate*, came to a similar conclusion. This time reproducing Mueller's account of the variegated thistle.

This wasn't the only time Mueller's writing for non-specialists was criticised for being overly technical. His manuscript of a textbook for use in schools was at the Government Printer when production was suddenly halted. 'On Ministerial request the author was induced to postpone the more extensive work on the native flora, in order that a smaller publication…should take precedence', wrote Mueller in the preface to that 'smaller publication', *Introduction to Botanic Teachings at the Schools of Victoria through References to Leading Native Plants* (1877). Although asked to abandon 'as much as ever possible scientific terms, names and appellations', if you flick though the pages of *Introduction to Botanic Teachings* you'll see plenty of pistils, cotyledons and Latin plurals that survived the redraft.

By all accounts Mueller was prone to coinage and idiosyncratic expression. And sometimes German syntax shadows his English like a novice spy. At some point, however, a botanical writer on a project like *Illustrated Thistles* has to become a translator, of science into prose the layperson understands. And Mueller could not. His sentences backfired, his vocabulary was opaque. A judgement reinforced by Alfred J. Ewart in 1909, when he complained of 'the cumbrous, involved and, to the farmer, more or less incomprehensible descriptions of the Thistle Pamphlet'.

*

Mueller's booklet was updated by agricultural scientist Alan Morgan from the Werribee State Research Farm. And reissued, probably in the late 1930s, as *Illustrated Description of Thistles, Etc., Included Within the Provisions of the Vermin and Noxious Weeds Act of 1928*. The new edition contained explanatory diagrams, condensed verbal portraits and a focus on control measures. It covered twenty-three thistles and allied plants, including the splendidly named 'purplish cornflower or terrible weed'. Ashley's original illustrations remained.

Thistles: Identification and Control appeared in 1946, reprinted from the Victorian Department of Agriculture's journal of that year. It is basically Morgan's earlier work with black and white photographs instead of coloured sketches, and two additional species, African thistle and oxtongue thistle.

*

Home. The English translation of *Heimat* falls short of the German concept. Nevertheless, the desire to belong is something we understand across the borders of language. In the same letter in which he mentions *Illustrated Thistles*, Hilgard (a fellow German) urges Mueller to revisit their native land. He never did.

Much has been written about Mueller's life and work. Most scholars acknowledge that, despite his considerable achievements, he wasn't always a popular figure. He fitted awkwardly into Anglo-Celtic Australia. Into Melbourne society.

I imagine him organising his office or out in the field; nights vast and spangled with stars.

He'd never set foot in England but in letters to William Hooker he referred to it as 'home' – as did British settlers.

I imagine him finding a home in science.

An enthusiastic acclimatiser, Mueller's most successful publication was *Select Extra-tropical Plants Readily Eligible for Industrial Culture or Naturalisation*. Earlier in the picture Darwin had sought his opinion about the ability of British and north European perennials to withstand the South Australian climate.

He was a man of Catholic interests.

An active supporter of the Melbourne Liedertafel, a choral group formed by German migrants and sojourners.

He waxed lyrical about sub-Antarctic islands; produced a monograph, *The Vegetation of the Chatham Islands*; and spoke about inducing 'some sturdy people' from the Shetlands and Scottish Highlands to settle on Macquarie Island.

In 1865 he gave a lecture: 'The fate of Leichhardt'. It was a dramatic presentation, a call to arms aimed at the ladies of the colony. He needed their fundraising skills and, voilà, the Ladies' Leichhardt Search Committee was born. Which sounds to me like the title of a play. Long skirts and pluck in the outback.

Obituaries applauded Mueller's diligence. And damned him with qualified praise.

'The value of his work consists largely in the fact that he did exactly the kind of work that was required in a young country for its material as well as its moral development. It is true that his work exhibits more industry than genius; but after all, what he undertook gave little scope for the latter quality.'

W. Bottong Hemsley, *Nature*, Volume 54, 1896.

The anonymously penned tribute in *The Gardeners'*
Chronicle recounted a few biographical highlights before
concluding that Mueller's vanity and desire for acclaim led
him to over-publish and indulge in vagaries of nomenclature.

*

Illustrated Thistles contains twelve colour plates. I find them
exquisite, but Mueller wasn't impressed. 'As the first effort
of an artist, who on this occasion had to be initiated into
plant-drawing, the coloured delineations now offered must
be regarded as fairly creditable.'

In the latter part of the nineteenth century,
chromolithography brought colour to the masses. Made
large-format printing affordable. Even so, in 1893 a dozen
illustrations represented a significant investment on the part
of the Department of Agriculture.

Luminous, evocative, *Illustrated Thistles* recalls a time when
craftsmen and women – painters, engravers, model makers,
taxidermists – went to extraordinary lengths in pursuit of
scientific accuracy. Along with portraits are montages of
details, some enlarged, some not. Here's a creeping thistle,
roots and all, with cutaways of its flower and fruit. Here's the
spear thistle, its leaves drawn life size.

These pictures may emphasise, perhaps exaggerate, the
thistles' formidable appearance but, for the non-specialist
trying to pinpoint an individual, they'd be far more helpful
than Mueller's text. It was language, not botanical art, that
consigned *Illustrated Thistles* to the mustiness of postscripts
and obscurity.

The pamphlet may be only a small piece of this immigrant
plant's Australian narrative. It may be one of Mueller's more
utilitarian works, but it glows with confidence that the

information it imparts is solid and important. It rejoices in the knowability of nature. But *Illustrated Thistles* also hints at cultural loss. A smartphone snap takes seconds; one of Ashley's plates took days of careful looking. Technology may have replaced chromolithographs with more advanced tools of visualisation. But there's something about those old images and the spaces around them where thoughts germinate and dreams flourish.

(WHAT THEY SAID ABOUT) STAR THISTLES

I
There are stars among thistles
quite a lot of them in fact.

Radio waves sing in the air.
Fade in appropriate music, and –
Let the show begin!

Jovial Host announces
the genus *Centaurea*
furnishes delightful garden plants,
the ever-popular cornflower
and other inoffensives,
but it also claims its share of weeds. Knapweeds and ——

A siren's voice approaches
raises the (dramatic) stakes.

Authorities yesterday issued a warning…

Star thistles are on the increase.
Centaurea calcitrapa – and that's just for starters.
Add rough star thistle,
Malta star thistle
and St Barnaby's or yellow star thistle to the mix.
All species of *Centaurea*.

Invited Expert explains

there's also the glaucous star thistle
and the false star thistle,
which belong to a different genus.

Interesting fact:
False star thistles are saffron thistles are *Carthamus lanatus*.
They appear in Governor King's March 1803 *List of Plants in the Colony of New South Wales that are not Indigenous*.
'Carthamus. Bastard Saffron. Scarce.'

Second (slightly junior) Expert expands
the background:
Saffron thistles have a history
of being referred to as star thistles even though they're not.

Cue mild surprise.

This error can be traced to the wording of an 1887 South Australian Act of Parliament to prevent the further spread of star thistles – although the plant the politicians had in their crosshairs was actually *Carthamus lanatus*. As both true and false star thistles were considered equally objectionable at the time, the misnomer was expedient.

It starts as habitat and becomes a story of sorts.
Mistakes accumulate like sediment
and solidify into specious IDs.

One of the difficulties with vernacular names is the paucity of suitable adjectives. How do you name thousands of plants from a vocabulary of a few hundred terms, many of which describe features common to dozens of species?

Jovial Host jumps in.

Switches to quiz mode:

Hollow crown, student and envy are varieties of parsnip. True or false?[2]

Question Two.

The aforementioned star thistles are all Mediterranean natives. True or false?

That's correct, Jess from Blackheath, they are.

Three.

As well as here and North America, Malta star thistle has naturalised on several Pacific islands.

Make waves
fade up
the swish of sickle
cutting through.

---

2   True. They are all varieties of parsnip.

II

In 1894 the New South Wales Department of Agriculture circulated a pamphlet: *The True Star Thistle.*

Its author, J. H. Maiden, wrote:

'This thistle seems to be execrated by everybody. In regard to most plants which are reported to be a nuisance, apologists find at least one redeeming feature in them, but I have never heard a good word put in for the Star Thistle. It is a vegetable outlaw, and every man's hand is against it, or would be, if it were not so prickly.'

It's true, we don't know much about this star thistle's journey
of migration to Australia,
but *Centaurea calcitrapa* was here by 1872.
Its ripe pink-purple flowers infiltrating,
generating concern.

First responders turn into open fields.
Crushed matter attached to wheels,
seed-heads, thistle-legs,
the bones of dying plants.

Add a breeze and the burr of a tractor to the mix.
Then back to the studio:
Q: What's almost a metre high, ends in a ball of needles, and is toxic to horses?
A: St Barnaby's or yellow star thistle.

Over to the Ecologist:
Star thistles are wasteland-growers
and disturbance specialists.
They live fast and die young
make seeds while the sun shines.

Weeds of roadsides and agricultural land.
They handle drought where others can't.

SFX. Construction broken up by rasps of static.

You see them spring up
around new housing tracts;
where acres of wildscape are cleared
the plants do what comes naturally.

From star down to thistle
developers crawl across country, devouring trees and grassland,
leaving suburbs that look like afterthoughts,
naming their droppings for the species they've displaced:
Ironbark Ridge, Saltbush Crescent, Currawong Drive.
You pass subdivisions and 7-Elevens,
preschools and swimming pools,
rubbish bins with haloes of flies.
Crows gather in the (car) park and you remember
this half-built housing estate near where you lived as a child.
A billboard declared: Tomorrow's Living for Today.
But somewhere along the road, money ran out –
the developer abandoned the venture, and for ages it remained,
brambles overgrowing,
a kind of outer suburban ruin. As if some tribe
of middle managers
had inexplicably come and gone.

Feedback.
Farmer Joe phones in: For years he's been troubled with star thistles.

A Listener tweets –
The words 'true' and 'false' orbit around star thistles.

Back to our quiz – and this is a tricky one:
Because star thistles are aggressive colonisers and establish quickly, they protect soil exposed by overgrazing, recreational activity, etc. Fact or fiction?

Here's a fact.
Facts aren't what they used to be.
That's why we lock more and more of them inside quotation marks.
And don't for a minute think star thistles are innocent – because they're not.

III
The audio is archival.
The hours get longer at this time of night...
One sheep, two sheep, three, and there goes a black sheep
counting backwards: Z, Y, X, W, V, U, T, S – are you listening?

Jovial Host announces
Episode Two, a different ensemble, more quizzing.

Towards the end of 1886 the South Australian Parliament
cranked up the debate
about star thistles.

The tick-tock of an earlier time –
when time took its time.

The Commissioner of Crown Lands begins:
'Cattle and sheep would not eat the star thistle; and on Mr
Magarey's run in the southeast, although there was plenty of
grass between the thistles, the sheep when he saw them were
nearly walking skeletons. The thistles stood up almost like
British bayonets.'

Mr Duncan:
'There could be no doubt as to the noxiousness of the star
thistle.'

Jovial Host reminds us
we're in repeat mode.
Almost a year later
the Star Thistle Destruction Bill –
the idea of it
was discussed.

Take it away!

Mr Holder speaks at length:
'It was a further evil to the pastoralists, inasmuch as it took the place of useful grass…Unless means were taken to eradicate it it would be spread far and wide and would not be of less importance than the rabbits and sparrows.'

Commissioner of Crown Lands:
'The Bill introduced by Mr Holder was a very important measure, and…not the first time this question of eradicating the star thistle had been brought under the notice of the honourable members.'

Chorus:
Hear, hear!

The Commissioner then reads a report from Dr Schomburgk, curator of the Adelaide Botanic Garden and a recognised authority.

Dr Schomburgk (heavy German accent):
'The star thistle, *Centaurea calcitrapa* ——'

Hoots of jokey blokey laughter.

Dr Schomburgk ploughs on:
'It is no doubt a very dangerous plant, and should be eradicated.'

Jovial Host interjects a contemporary note:
Saucy Jack, Wild Irishman and Cockspur are all common names for the Malta star thistle. True or false?

Interesting fact:
According to Dr Schomburgk's 1897 booklet, *On the Naturalised Weeds and other Plants in South Australia*, the Malta star thistle 'was introduced as far back as 1844'.

Another interesting fact:
J. H. Maiden again. This time *The Weeds of New South Wales*. Writing about the saffron or false star thistle, he points out that its name is doubly deceptive. It's neither a true star thistle, nor does it have anything to do with saffron the spice. In some districts the plant is known as Chinese or yellow Chinese thistle. 'But the Mongolians are not responsible for its introduction.'

To keep listeners tuned in
and because some things are better explored through fiction
a Special Guest takes up the story with both hands,
unfolds it carefully, like origami.
In spring she listened to the creek's falling song and prayed for clouds. Driving along a dirt trail in summer she looked through the scrim of dust at rows of grain whipping past. At tractors pushing their own shadows. Thistles grinding against blue relentless sky. What became of the boy with the wheatshock hair? Olive who bred donkeys? The old piano and the hours spent sitting beside her father as he taught her to play. His workman hands nimble over the keys; hers forever hitting the wrong notes.

Back to the pitter-pat of parliamentary dialogue.
September 1887
Mr Caldwell felt it was 'his duty to oppose the Bill'.
He wasn't a fan of legislation,
the star thistle was not especially troublesome –

arguments ping-ponged
about the plant's menace
about its value as forage.

Mr Howe:
'would be the last one in the world to destroy any weed
which might be useful to either man or beast, especially in a
country like this, where we were visited very often by seasons
of drought.'
The creak of old wood,
assorted coughing.
From outside the chamber
Wie schön leuchete der Morgenstern...
the distant echo of a hymn.

'He had never seen any one who thought the Bathurst burr
a necessary weed, and he classed the star thistle in the same
category; in fact of the two he would prefer the Bathurst burr.'

The Honourable G. C. Hawker:
'considered it one of the vilest weeds ever introduced into
the colony.'

Jovial Host pushes the point:
The vilest weed the land ever produced.

Thursday 8 September 1887
the Star Thistle Destruction Bill
Passed its third reading.

A select committee gathered
so that honourable members might not
be moving altogether in the dark.

The rustle of scripts
the scratch of the minute-taker's pen.

Legislative Council, Friday 9 December 1887.
Cue regal trumpets.
His Excellency in the name of Her Majesty Queen Victoria,
assented to the following –
Star Thistle Destruction Bill.

SFX. Wild track:
Wind. The suck of stream on shingle.

The hours get longer at this time of night…
One sheep, two sheep, three, four – are you listening?
The problem is the stars
keep shifting position in their herds.

WAR

SOLDIER THISTLE

I

Linneaus was confused or hedging his bets: was it *Carduus* or *Cnicus acarna*? But he wasn't the only botanist bemused by this thistle. The eighteenth century saw a lot of taxonomic toing and froing and the plant we know today as *Picnomon acarna* collected its share of synonyms and classification claims.

In 1570 the plant was identified by Mathias de L'Obel and Pierre Pena as *Picnomos Cretæ Salonensis*:

'A small, attractive and rare thistle growing on the dry coastal plain between the ancient cities of Arles and Salon-de-Provence.'

Their description unfurls in long, multiple-clause sentences that exceed the *amo, amas, amant* of my remembered school Latin – even with the aid of a dictionary and Google Translate.

The assertions are granular.
Leaves spread in defence
of this or that system.
L'Obel broke with tradition and based his plant families on the form of their leaves, rather than their medicinal utility.
Under the glassy stare of the Rare Book Room
an illustration of *Picnomos Cretæ Salonensis*.
With its arrangement of leaves the scientists call alternate and lobed (slightly).

We could meander through the taxonomic maze, but let's instead leapfrog to 1826 and Frédéric Cuvier's *Dictionnaire des science naturelles.* When the botanical community settled on the name *Picnomon acarna*. Give or take the occasional outlier.

II

'During the last year or two a new thistle has made its appearance in the country near Sellick Hill and down towards Myponga and the sea coast. This is the *Picnomon Acarna*, which, from its erect growth and formidable spines, has received the local name of "Soldier Thistle." Like so many of the alien plants which take kindly to our soil and clime, it comes from the Mediterranean region. Fortunately, it is only an annual, and is not, therefore, likely to prove very troublesome, although our experience with it is still so limited that it would be rash to express any decided opinion.'

The Journal of the Department of Agriculture of South Australia, August 1907 – July 1908.

That paragraph from April 1908 is the first record of the plant in Australia. Published more or less verbatim in a handful of newspapers the same year. In 1909 soldier thistle appeared in J. M. Black's *The Naturalised Flora of South Australia*.

In technical prose.

And line drawing.

A full-frontal thistle.

*

Although the seeds of *Picnomon acarna* can be transferred by animals and machinery, wind is their main means of dispersal. Early autumn when the thistles die, their skeletons become brittle. Sometimes on a blustery day, whole plants break off at the base and go rolling around as tumbleweeds.

Come winter, new-generation seedlings erupt from the earth like tiny grey-green stars.

Come spring, the soldier thistle finds a kick of speed. Rosette growth is rapid and by the start of summer the plant is in full bloom – although here the expression 'full bloom' is somewhat misleading. *Picnomon acarna*'s pink florets are small, nestled deep in the inflorescence, and modest compared to the showy flowerings of, say, artichoke or Scotch thistles.

A weed of waysides, irrigation ditches and degraded areas, soldier thistles favour semi-arid terrain and sandy or stony soils. Initially confined to parts of South Australia, the plant spread across state lines to inland and western Victoria. In January 1940 the Victorian government proclaimed it noxious under section 6 of the Vermin and Noxious Weeds Act of 1928.

'Soldier Thistle is an obnoxious pest mainly on account of its prickly nature…Owing to its deeply penetrating root system, this weed robs the soil of valuable nutrients and moisture to the detriment of useful species.'

The Journal of the Department of Agriculture of South Australia again. This time a profile from 1955.

III

In Turkey and Lebanon *Picnomon acarna* is a common – and unwelcome – presence along roads and railway lines, around airports and in cereal fields.

Among the chickpeas,

and sunflower crops,

its prickly legions.

Soldier thistle's native range circles the Mediterranean basin and runs as far east as Kazakhstan. Even in their homelands, indigenous species can be deemed unwanted weeds.

Beyond its native range the thistle has naturalised only in Afghanistan and Australia.

*

As pests go it's not even B-list; it's a lesser, low down, way down the list weed. A minor character, a bit part player.

Remember: there are no small roles, only small actors.

That mantra is attributed to the Russian theatre director Stanislavsky.

The reality is this: in film and television a bit part is a role with no more than fifty words of dialogue. The bit part player is further down the food chain than a supporting actor, but above an extra.

Occasionally a bit part is a trigger or in some other way important in the storyline. Take that famous three-and-a-half minute opening shot of Orson Welles's 1958 film *Touch of Evil*.

In a Mexican border town, a bomb is planted in a parked convertible. Linnekar, an American businessman, and nightclub dancer Zita leave the bar and drive towards the US frontier. To a mélange of be-bop and Latin rhythms the camera tracks their car down streets alive with hawkers, goats and shadowy figures. At the checkpoint – where these bit parters briefly cross paths with the film's lead characters – Zita insists she can hear ticking:

'Hey, hey, I got this – I got this ticking noise – no, really, this ticking noise in my head.'

Their car crosses the border. Then explodes in flames.

Theatre's definition of a bit part is more relaxed. Shakespeare's plays abound with miscellaneous Messengers, Musicians, Nurses, Gravediggers, Gaolers, Watchmen and Second Murderers. Modern productions usually snip out the majority of these roles with any remaining small parts shared among the cast who double – and triple.

These days a cast of six is considered large. Not for commercial musicals of course, but for subsidised and independent theatre. Outside the community or youth sectors, opportunities for contemporary dramatists to give our large-cast playwriting muscles a workout are scarce. On a more cheerful note, although creating scripts for non-professional performers involves constraints, it also offers the freedom to sidestep the polarities of Stars and Second Spear-carriers and write for an ensemble where pretty much everyone who wants to can appear on stage.

Called extras, supernumeraries, background actors or simply background, these are the uncredited people you see in crowd scenes, in queues, filling TV courtrooms and hospital waiting areas. They are the blurred bodies in the back of the restaurant where the leads are having their first fight. Before CGI (computer-generated images), war films often featured hundreds of background artists, sometimes literally a cast of thousands. Now, instead of hiring huge numbers of extras dressed up as warriors to charge across a floodplain, why not hire fifty and create a digital horde?

Two areas of modern life where feudal hierarchies persist are air travel and the film set. Leading actors are the kings and queens whose every command must be obeyed no matter how frivolous. Extras are cattle class.

Common or garden.

Suckers.

Ferals.

Chaff.

Weeds.

IV

What the soldier thistle lacks in dramatic backstory, it makes up for in spikiness. The plant is covered with yellow marginal spines, hence its alternative names yellow-spine, yellow-plume or just plain yellow thistle. Less obvious is how it came to be called soldier thistle in Australia. Several sources suggest it is because of *Picnomon acarna*'s upright bearing and heavy armament of sharp spines. It can withstand the vicissitudes of the environment. Survive the depredations of its enemies.

Maybe that *is* the origin of its name, but I can't help speculating. This may simply be my playwright's impulse to develop a counternarrative, but here goes:

April 1908, the thistle had been around for a couple of years. That takes us back to 1906. On 31 May 1902 the Boer War ended and Australian troops returned home from South Africa.

To the British, southern Africa was just another far-flung outpost of empire. Until prospectors chanced upon rich deposits of diamonds and gold. The Boer – Anglo-Boer or South African – War was about access to those resources. The British wanted control of the mines and in October 1899 they went to war with the Dutch-Afrikaner settlers to get it. British forces were supported by volunteer contingents from the colonies.

'Australasians and Canadians much in request for South Africa.'
The Mercury, Hobart, December 1899.

After Britain, Australia provided the largest number of troops.

There were a few dissenting voices, but a newspaper report of a packed public meeting in Toowoomba's Theatre Royal captured the prevailing mood.

Speeches were applauded.

British anthems sung with gusto.

Verses by Rudyard Kipling recited:

'...Will you kindly drop a shilling in my little tambourine

For a gentleman in khaki going South?'

In other towns and suburbs similar gatherings and fundraising drives were being organised. Enthusiasm for Australia's participation in the South African War was widespread.

'There might be blood shed in the Transvaal, but if it cemented the Rose, Shamrock, and Thistle, and the Stars and Stripes of America, then those who fell in the Transvaal would have fallen in a noble cause.'

Darling Downs Gazette, December 1899.

*

Unless you have a particular interest in it, or you're into the minutiae of military history (a field of limited appeal to female researchers – or so it seems), the Boer War is a few names on a memorial, a passing reference, a grainy snapshot. Eclipsed by World War I and without the romantic rah-rah of battles like Austerlitz, Waterloo or Custer's Last Stand. Yet upwards of 16,000 and maybe as many as 20,000 Australians served in the South African War. It was a big thing, in other words.

Could this be a factor in the story

of How the Soldier Thistle Got its Name?

In 1906 when the thistle was first noticed, memories of the conflict were still raw. There would have been a lot of returned servicemen seeking work – and a lot of frustration, as this letter to the editor reveals:

'When they left these shores they were given a splendid

send-off, and what were they promised by the Government? I will remind a few who may have forgotten some of the statements made. It was said that men who were leaving for the seat of war to represent South Australia, when they returned would be given situations…

On behalf of the returned contingent members,

Sergeant S. Kalman, Late First Kitchener's Fighting Scouts.'

The Advertiser, Adelaide, July 1902.

Three years later the issue and the outrage remained:

'Many of our returned soldiers gave up good employment and sacrificed home comforts, leaving behind all that was near and dear, and went to South Africa to bear the country's burden, with all its perils, and what return have many of them received? They find their places filled up, often by hungry aliens, and that there is no room for them…

I am, &c.,

Disgusted.'

The Advertiser, Adelaide, July 1905.

Recruits, irregulars, rank and file,
dime a dozen, ten a penny.
One, two, left, right,
line up to be knocked down.
Toy soldiers placed in commanded positions:
They can stand their ground or lie.
And when the battle is done
they'll be scooped up and laid to rest
in a box.

Toy soldiers, tin soldiers, foot soldiers –
Soldier thistles?

Although, as I said before, aligning the local name for this thistle and the Boer War may be nothing more than a wild fantasy.

*

A tangent of sorts: because I didn't grow up or go to school in Australia, my history of this country is patchy and partisan. I was vaguely aware of the 1980 Bruce Beresford film *Breaker Morant*; vaguely aware the action was set during the Boer War; vaguely aware the titular character was based on a real person. I've since done some reading and learnt a few biographical facts about Harry 'Breaker' Morant. Roustabout; military officer; most likely married, albeit briefly, to anthropologist Daisy Bates; writer of bush ballads – and war criminal. He confessed to the summary execution of nine prisoners of war. And was responsible for the slaughter of others, including civilians and a missionary who witnessed the massacre. Why does Australia make folk heroes of all the wrong people? Of killers and criminals? Look at the popularity of films, television series and books about them. Semi-fictionalised stories about thugs; ghost-written paperbacks; memoirs by the wives and girlfriends of thugs. How do we explain that fascination? I mean, a knockabout larrikin is one thing; a cold-blooded murderer is altogether something else.

Here's an idea: along with the male combatants who sailed to South Africa went more than sixty Australian nurses. One of their number, Sister Frances 'Fanny' Hines, was the first Australian woman to die on operational service. Let's honour her instead.

V

I'm no apologist for Kipling who was, yes, an apologist for England and empire, but I do like the performative nature of his poetry. His nods to vaudeville humour; his orchestration of voices; his centre-staging of rhythm, even if those imperial boots were 'foot – slog – slog – slog – sloggin' over Africa ——'.

The difficulties experienced by soldiers when they re-entered civilian life was a recurring theme for Kipling.

'Peace is declared, an' I return

To 'Ackneystadt, but not the same…'

What's worse: to be at war or to be at peace after having been at war?

'A fit country for heroes to live in', was the promise of Britain's Lloyd George in November 1918. A sentiment echoed by Australia's Prime Minister Hughes.

The immediate concern was to supply jobs for the quarter-million repatriated soldiers coming home to an Australia very different from the one they left. Legislation was passed designed to assist their transition. They were granted preferential employment in the public sector. Soldier Settlement Schemes were established not only to create opportunities for ex-servicemen to earn an income, but also with the broader aim of opening up new land for agriculture and boosting the country's rural economy. These schemes were not a success. The yeoman ideal didn't translate. Many of the allocated plots were unviable – too small or too marginal. Many of those who took up the offer had no experience of farming or of life in the bush. Weeds were a continual problem, as were rabbits. And isolation.

*

Thistle inspectors were employed by local councils to enforce the rulings of the various Thistle acts. Ensure landowners and tenants cleared thistles and other prohibited flora from their property. If they didn't, and legal proceedings followed, the inspectors would be called upon to give evidence for the prosecution. After World War I, there was a strong push to appoint returned servicemen wherever possible.

'Applications from Returned Soldiers will be received at the Shire Office, Bruthen, till noon of Tuesday, the 4th September, 1917, for the position of Summoning Officer, Inspector of Slaughteryards and Nuisances, Thistle Inspector, Dog Registrar, Herdsman, Receiver of Skins and Sanitary Collector, at a salary of £135 per annum.

Applications to be addressed to the President, Shire Office, Bruthen, and should be accompanied by Certificate of Discharge.'

Bruthen and Tambo Times, Victoria, August 1917.

Although I'd question the wisdom of exposing recent veterans to the blood and guts of a slaughteryard, reading the minutes of council meetings from several Victorian districts (the state with the most thistle inspectors), I'm touched by the level of community concern for these men. Time and again councillors reiterate the moral obligation to provide paid work for those who fought in the trenches. In some instances, the incumbent inspector volunteers to step aside so a former soldier can take his job.

*

'He started up in terror. What did he see? The plate of bananas on the sideboard. Nobody was there...

He was alone with the sideboard and the bananas. He was

alone, exposed on this bleak eminence, stretched out – but not on a hill-top; not on a crag; on Mrs Filmer's sitting-room sofa. As for the visions, the faces, the voices of the dead, where were they?'

The 'He' in that quotation from Virginia Woolf's 1925 novel, *Mrs Dalloway,* is Septimus Smith, a war-damaged veteran who dictates splintered, nonsensical poems to his wife, Rezia.

Shell shock.
Combat fatigue.
War of nerves.
PTSD.
Post-Traumatic Stress Disorder. Words with the ring of psychiatric authority. They give the impression medical science is coming to grips with the condition. A condition the collective mind associates with the legacy of the Vietnam War. Or is it just a more sciencey sounding title for a composite problem?

VI

CAST

Alice Robson, a suburban wife aged twenty-six.
Archie Robson, her husband, a war veteran aged twenty-eight.

ACT 1

The city. The Robson house.

ALICE

Imagine the soldier home from war:
Yoo-hoo he calls, striding in the back door.
Baggage not so lightweight behind him.
The hours spread out.
Days stumble along, fruitcake cut in slices, questions cut off
before they're asked.
Friends and neighbours give us a wide berth –
'You need time to yourselves.'
'Get to know each other again.'

He likes real butter and ham on the bone
An extra layer of jam.
The table between us
we eat in silence.

Imagine the soldier home from war:
Awkward, short of breath,
Thoughts chasing each other across his face like cloud
shadows.
Occasionally other ex-soldiers drop by. They do the polite
please-and-thank-you number –
'Hello, Alice, are you keeping well?'
'How's things on the home front?'

But when they're here, I feel like I don't belong. Like they've all come from a place where I don't exist.
Men see action. We peer thought gaps in the curtains and imagine disaster.

Sour corners, nicked edges,
An embroidered cloth goes over the top
to hide the tell-tale knocks and scratches
the cupboard has collected.
On the runner sit postcard mountains, bits and bobs, a newspaper cutting:
'A splendid range of Farms and subdivided Estates for Sale…
to Returned Soldiers…The terms are easy; the land is good…
You struck for liberty when you enlisted; strike now for individual liberty and prosperity. Get a farm of your own.'

I've asked him to clear out the shed and sort things
into useful and useless.
So I can spend the afternoon composing
a treacle tart – Archie's favourite, used to be.
That Christmas Eve, our first as marrieds, carols sweetening the air, kisses landing on flushed cheeks.
And me, full of piss and vinegar, eager to make a splash, impress the rellies with my cooking.

I've asked him about the war, course I have, loads of times.
Usually he doesn't answer, just sits there, gazing out the window. Thinking about something he'll never tell.
Sometimes I wonder
if the gunfire hasn't blasted the memories out of his head.
But this one time he surprises me when I ask:
What was it really like over there?
Like theatre, he says. From the audience you see a carefully

constructed stage set and actors make-believing the lines they're speaking are true. But behind the scenes there's broken frames and rusted nails and wood scraps and cigarette butts and cockroaches. There's no magic; it's dark as boots and filthy.

While he's in the garden doing a spot of weeding, I sit in the kitchen and read recipes. Between raspberry buns and royal icing I think about the brief flutter of time we have to be young.
There's a sudden scream and then shouting: snake behind the compost heap! He's killed it, and now he's scything down thistles and dandelion clocks and – No! – the snapdragons, the passionfruit vine, potato plants – everything in the garden that was roses.

Beat.

Last week it was the cicadas that set him off.
Like nightmares follow day.
Oh, Archie, don't lose it. Hang on, hang on to me, hang on to hope, to reason. Don't let the experience crush the joy out of you and leave you desolate.

Imagine the soldier home from war:
A shipwreck in a bottle,
Spread out over papers or cleaning his gun.
While I tell the story I'm good at: you just need time, that's all. To settle in, get used to things…No, I'm not crying, it's the onions.

Until finally it comes, our fresh start, our new life
on the land.
A letter official-stamped: To Mr and Mrs Archie Robson.

ACT 2
The country. The Robson house.
Three months later.

ALICE
Well, here we are:
Unpacking – done.
Open accounts – done.
Meet the locals – done.
Here we are:
Where the land gives up its grain and dust rises along the horizon like a huge planet out of orbit.
Shrubs that barely raise themselves above ground. Dirt roads that lead nowhere. A million thistles.

Archie told everybody this move was a good thing – for us, for him – and it is, it will be…
But the fear remains.
He wakes in the middle of the night drenched in sweat, shaking –
Then he's ashamed for being afraid. He survived the trenches, but here in the middle of nowhere, a dog's bark sends his heart racing.
I lead him from flashback to bed
No more talk. Let me put you to sleep.

Beat.

I remember when the days had a skip in them.
I remember our hands grubbing through the dry grass
for each other…

After supper he gets lost within calling distance,

And the darkness that's deeper than the heavens falls down over the house.
I make an appointment with the doctor in town. He talks in straight lines, but I've come to think life follows untidier arcs.
I buy a dozen wide-mouth jars, go home and read up on the art of stewing.

Beat.

Podding peas,
Rolling pastry in front of an open book –
Pastry can be flaky,
short, suet, hot water,
puff and rough puff.

Imagine soldiers home from war:
They aren't regular men any more.
And we're trying to heal them, treating them like heroes and children at the same time.
After a while no one comes to check on us –
'Just popping in to say hello.'
'If there's anything you need...'
I get under the blanket with Archie and fall asleep. When I wake up, for just that first moment I think I'm back at our old house in the city.
There's a muddy dam spuming with yabbies, but overall the place has an air of exhaustion, as though it's been baked into silence by the unclouded sun.
It's strange, this huge silence, devoid of people. I'm such a city mouse, I've only ever seen silence in photographs.

Beat.

It's not the blood clots or the fear or shame.

Beat.

It's the anger that eats away at the seams of our couplehood until we fall apart.

VII

At some point in humankind's so-called war on weeds, we declared war on metaphor. And waged that war until we wrote and talked about our relationship with unwanted flora almost solely in combat terms. Don't believe me? Read the evidence:

'Ministers surrender in battle to eradicate Japanese knotweed.'
The Telegraph, UK, July 2015.

'Winning the weeds battle with a no-survivors policy.'
The Australian Cottongrower, August–September 2014.

'We are under attack. An alien is overrunning our gardens and breaking into our homes – cracking concrete foundations, smashing through brickwork and rearing up between floorboards. The invader is Japanese knotweed... [and an entomologist] is mounting a counter-offensive.'
New Scientist, July 2014.

'Growers given ammunition to fight weed enemies.'
Australian Government Grains Research and Development Corporation, May 2012.

'War on weeds loses ground.'
Nature, May 2012.

'Green groups call for war on weeds.'
The Age, Melbourne, May 2009.

'Forces unite in war against weeds.'
Landline, ABC (Australia), November 2001.

'This year, a growing number of homeowners who consider themselves peaceable will once again "arm" themselves to wage war on weeds.'
The Cedartown Standard, USA, August 1993.

'Declare War. The country is besieged by Woody Weeds. Do your bit.' Advertisement for herbicides in *The Times* from Victor Harbor, South Australia, November 1988.

'The war on weeds has been waged for centuries with no truce in nearly every country of the world, but the battle continues to grow with each breath of Spring.'
The Aberdeen Times, USA, September 1973.

*

Weeds have defied humankind for millennia. Folklore, proverbs and Biblical parables all speak of our encounters with 'the idle weeds that grow/ In our sustaining corn' (*King Lear*). Why did we start using militaristic language to frame our interactions? When did hawkish metaphors become the norm? World War II was my first thought. End of, to be specific. Because that year saw the unleashing of technologies that completely and forever changed the parameters of warfare. The United States dropped atomic bombs on the Japanese cities of Hiroshima and Nagasaki while, on the home front, brand-new chemical weedkillers hit the market.

February 1945. An article in *Time* magazine announced that 'US farmers and gardeners are better armed than ever before for this year's battles against their prime enemies – insects and weeds'.

That same month *Better Homes & Gardens* made explicit the enemy parallel: 'Toughest of all weeds to control are the deep-rooted perennials – bindweed, Canada thistle, burdock, dandelion – gangster weeds that thrust roots deep into moist soil and dig in like trapped Japs in pillboxes. And in the past, like Japs, the only way they could be destroyed was to root them out.'

A bit more archival digging, however, and you soon discover that the roots of this linguistic defeat go back further than 1945. 'Agriculture is a perpetual conflict with aggressive plants' was the opening sentence of an 1872 American publication, *A Manual of Weeds, or the Weed Exterminator*. Three years later a Brisbane newspaper reported: 'An association for the purposes of making continuous war upon thistles and other grass destroyers has been established on the Downs.'

'Thirteen years of thistle invasion.'

In 1923 a regional New South Wales newspaper described saffron thistles growing so thickly on the local Soldier Settlement that a councillor 'had to send his mowing machine to cut a track through the thistles to enable the settlers' wives to get from their cottages to their clothes lines'.

Sometimes, though, this combative lexicon yields incongruous almost-poetry. 'War on buttercups' was the oxymoronic title of a syndicated snippet from 1927.

*

When weeds disrupt our garden designs, agricultural enterprise, our plans for biodiversity conservation, the first instinct is to retaliate. Forget peaceful coexistence, much easier to go the knee-jerk route and deploy the vocabulary of the battlefield. Words that appeal to gut feelings. Words that shout action. Words repeated so often they lodge in the collective cerebral cortex and acquire the guise of universal knowledge.

We.

Us.

Our.

The pronouns are plural, suggesting common ground and shared experience, but the arguments are subjective.

'Experts battling thistle invasion in the M.I.A. [Murrumbidgee Irrigation Area].'
Daily Advertiser, New South Wales, October 1954.

Opportunistic, noxious, pernicious, injurious – a few of the adjectives attached to plants demonised as weeds. Until the middle of the last century, noxious was probably the favoured term, at least in Australia. That changed. Now heartlands and waste corners, the pages of specialist journals and conference keynotes are full of invasive species. And invasion is not a neutral term. It reeks of crisis, of border protection and lines crossed. It has nationalistic overtones. It engenders fear.

'Sir Joseph Hooker was fond of pointing out that none of the destructive agencies on the earth's surface is, in the aggregate, comparable to those of plants, and I suppose the veteran would have repeated these remarks even if he had known of the orgy of devastation caused by the Great War.' Those sombre words come from J. H. Maiden's lecture, 'The economic aspect of the weed problem', delivered to the August 1919 meeting of the Royal Society of New South Wales.

Picture the assembly rooms at 5 Elizabeth Street, Sydney, that winter evening. High ceilings, an expanse of Persian carpet, maybe a geological model of this or that mountain range, its crevasses collecting dust. Portraits of leading men on the walls. Stories in marble and stone. Big whiskery ideas. And an audience of what? Forty, fifty men. And they would have been men because the Society didn't admit women members until 1935.

Although invasion biology didn't emerge as a formally defined field until the early 1980s, Charles Elton, de facto father of the subdiscipline, began his seminal 1958 work, *The Ecology of Invasions by Animals and Plants*, with images of war: 'It is not just nuclear bombs and wars that threaten us... there are other sorts of explosions, and this book is about ecological explosions.'

*

Again. Why have martial analogies come to dominate the conversation about unwelcome plants? I think there are several answers to that question. Here are four of them:

Weeds challenge our sense of entitlement.

'The earth was given us to subdue and occupy. Unless we do subdue we cannot occupy, and if an enemy come in to contest the conquest with us after it is made, we must fight for our possession...The thistle may be considered a hardship, and be looked at gloomily as another of the barriers found in this colony between the colonist and the "fortune" he comes to snatch', declared *The Sydney Mail and New South Wales Advertiser* in 1871.

Possessive pronouns work like this:

We have a plot.

The lot belongs to us.

It's our patch.

This land is ours –

Nine-tenths of the law.

The article concluded with the example of South Australia, where 'the thistle was the subject of an Act of Parliament...

soldiers were engaged upon the roads in spudding it, and soon dispatched the invader in bloodless battle'.

Two. Weeds defy narrow utilitarian worldviews.

'If weeds were of much value as food either for man or beast, there would not be the same necessity for waging against them, a war of extermination.'

Weeds and How to Eradicate Them by Thomas Shaw, Canada, 1893.

Three. There is a popular belief that the best way to solve a problem is to go in guns blazing. And hope for the best when the smoke clears. And let's not forget there are vested interests involved. The business of killing weeds is a very profitable one. Talking up the threat of bellicose botanical invaders diverts attention from collateral damage caused when herbicides run off, leach into waterways and drift onto food crops. Camouflages the gap between facts and values by pretending there are only facts.

Four. Military metaphors are performative. They raise the stakes. They conscript humankind and floral marauders into a full-blown drama. An old-fashioned hero-and-villain narrative where tradition dictates the hero will (eventually) be victorious.

How vexing then if weeds don't play their part as written.

VIII

'The war on weeds is a real one, a grim struggle for existence.'
Auckland Star, New Zealand, October 1925.

Except it's not, is it? The war on weeds isn't a war. There is no conflict. The antagonist or enemy isn't hostile towards us. Weeds are the foe not because of anything intrinsic to the plants themselves, but because of our desire to eliminate them. It's a one-sided set-up.

Weeds happen.

'It's just about time for another re-enactment of that epic conflict. The annual battle of the weeds.'
Northwest Columbus News, USA, May 2004.

That quote prompts images of mock battles and the armies of weekend hobbyists who recreate historical skirmishes from Agincourt to the American Civil War and beyond. Maybe one day we'll see people dressing up in protective overalls with goggles and respirators to re-enact the Blitz on Weeds?

If the linguistic war on weeds has become more belligerent, something of the reverse has happened to media coverage of actual wars. Shocking events are described in dispassionate syntax, concealed under acronyms or euphemisms that shade the truth and put a comfortable distance between us and violence. Some of the footage looks more like a video game than it does the frontline. And weeds aren't alone:

We have wars on crime and cancer.

On poverty.

Graffiti.

'Metaphors are the dreamwork of language', wrote American philosopher Donald Davidson in his classic 1978 essay.

Metaphors may be the ghostwork of language but they also have consequences in the real world. They colour our thinking and frame debate. Why must each cause, each concerted effort be compared to warfare? If we label every campaign from reducing litter to tackling childhood obesity a war, don't we downgrade the horror of bombardment and slaughter? When we talk about waging war against weeds aren't we endorsing the logic of the battleground? Like the war on terror and the war on drugs, the war on weeds misuses the military metaphor. It oversimplifies a complicated issue. Let's save our fighting words for real wars with real victims.

Weeds have happened.

Will continue to happen.

If we're going to adapt to living in these novel ecosystems we need to revise our figurative language. We may need a whole new playbook. I think we certainly need what Canadian scholar Brendon Larson calls 'sustainable metaphors'.

There are other ways to focus community attention besides a call to arms. Here's an example from 1920:

'If the farmer were to look for an hotel-keeper willing to board him indefinitely for nothing, he would look for a long time: if he were to seek one willing to board him and to regard his presence with philosophy while he elbowed paying boarders off the verandah's pleasantest spots and sprawled in the best chairs, he would look still longer. Yet (say officers of the Department of Agriculture), many farmers adopt the attitude of such a host in their ultra-hospitable attitude to weeds. Good land costs money, and every plant that stretches out roots for food should be at least a little more than paying for its keep.'

Manilla Express, New South Wales.

IX

The idea of enemy agents planted in an unsuspecting community, agents who may at some stage perform hostile acts, has been – and remains – a source of deep anxiety. These operatives are known as sleeper agents or moles. Spies who infiltrate a target country or organisation and bide their time. Acquire identities as regular citizens with regular jobs, blend in, don't communicate with other agents and do nothing to attract unwanted attention. They have no immediate mission other than to lie low and maintain a normal life, sometimes for years.

As far as I can tell, the phrase 'sleeper weeds' came into use in the 1990s.

'One thing we can learn from history is that most of today's bad weeds sat around for years, for decades often, before erupting as major problems. The lesson is that further such "sleepers" are almost certainly out there...'
Use With Care: Managing Australia's Natural Resources in the Twenty-first Century by Doug Cocks, 1992.

And this from a paper presented at the Twelfth Australian Weeds Conference in 1999. Sleeper weeds are 'those invasive plants that have naturalised in a region but not yet increased their population size exponentially'.

For me, the first of those two quotations conjures not so much weediness as Cold War scenes filmed in black and white with long lenses and tracking shots. Twilight zones of rain and fog; clandestine rendezvous featuring men in bulky overcoats.

The early hours of a damp and chill November morning.

A Mercedes slowly approaches the Heerstraße checkpoint that separates West Berlin from its communist twin. Border guards stand alert in the dawn haze. From the hinterland of East Germany comes a second vehicle. Prisoners are exchanged. The cars depart the way they came.

Sleeper weeds may appear benign for long periods then spread rapidly following some kind of environmental disturbance: bushfire, a shift in land use, drought or deluge. Climate change is also a factor. How will it affect the behaviour of these slumbering species?

Lurking weeds.

Plants just waiting to go feral.

A new suite of plant invaders.

While it has gained traction in certain quarters, among scholars 'sleeper weeds' is a questionable category – verging on propaganda, according to some. 'Government agencies should not engage in psychological warfare against their own citizens as part of their war on weeds', wrote John Dwyer, advocate for more measured language in the troublesome taxa debate.

Eighteenth Australasian Weeds Conference, 2012.

Sleeper agents are popular in film and fiction. Mole was a term used by John Le Carré in his 1974 novel, *Tinker, Tailor, Soldier, Spy*. A tale of efforts to uncover a Soviet mole in the upper echelons of the British Secret Intelligence Service.

Mole: an operative who slowly but surely works his or her way to a vital position within an organisation.

In the 1962 film *The Manchurian Candidate* a brainwashed Korean War hero is programmed into a communist sleeper. His assignment: to assassinate a presidential candidate.

Once upon a lunchtime in Seoul, in the staff refectory at

the university where I had a writing residency, I got chatting with a colleague. I'd been to North Korea the previous month – a place off-limits to the majority of Southerners. This colleague, let's call him Professor Choi, was interested in espionage.

'There are hundreds of deep-cover agents in this country,' he said.

'North Korean spies?'

'Mostly.'

A good spy is a face in the crowd, invisible – like a ghost, he told me. They have the uncanny ability to pass unnoticed, even if they juggle tins of tuna in the supermarket queue or tap dance in the subway. They know how to pick out the important words from the common barrage.

X

In 2003 the Commonwealth Bureau of Rural Sciences shortlisted a number of potential agricultural sleeper weeds. One of the nominated plants was Taurian thistle. Isolated pockets of *Onopordum tauricum* were recorded at sites in regional Victoria, and the species is believed to have been present at one of those locations prior to the outbreak of World War I. There was also an unsubstantiated report of Taurian thistle from South Australia. Like a number of other introduced thistles, it's a native of southeastern Europe. Unlike its compatriots, it isn't widespread. Its antipodean population remains small, its distribution localised. Weed managers and agronomists have nonetheless recommended eradication. *Onopordum* is a large genus whose species frequently hybridise. What if Taurian thistle were to come in contact with a related *Onopordum*?

i.e., Scotch,

Illyrian

or stemless thistles.

Is it a sleeper weed that could one day wake up and wreak havoc?

XI

One of the best-known examples of delayed spread is the escape of Oxford ragwort from the University Botanic Garden. Despite its vernacular name, *Senecio squalidus* is indigenous to Sicily. By the early eighteenth century, the daisy with its straggly yellow flowers was established in the Garden. (Joseph Banks noticed it there in the 1770s.) Following many years' uneventful cultivation in the herbaceous borders, by the mid-1800s the downy seeds had reached the city's railway line. By the middle of the next century this once-scarce plant was on its way to ubiquity in England and Wales. Bomb damage from World War II and a program of motorway construction created new habitats for the ragwort. And the rest, as they say, is history.

Which brings us back to the books.

The kind of books where a story that begins in the Caucasus has its final act in London. The concourse of Liverpool Street Station. Watery sunlight trickles through glass panels in its vaulted roof. The 10.32 train from Cambridge pulls in. A newspaper-seller approaches one of the disembarking passengers. A dark sedan parked nearby speeds off...

XII

'I know only one species of Acarna', wrote French botanist Sébastien Vaillant in 1718.

Wikipedia concurs: 'The only known species is *Picnomon acarna*.'

The crucial word in these sentences is 'known'. Taxonomic choreography is ongoing; at some point in the future could scientists shuffle in a second or third species? Or even better, discover a totally new one?

Picnomon comes from the Greek *pyknos,* meaning either bitter or compact, and *nomos,* pasture. The *acarna* probably refers to Acarnania, a region of central-west Greece. It's a thistle-word you often see in herbals and historical texts; a class of its own in one of my favourite tomes, Parkinson's *Theatrum Botanicum* (Theatre of Plants).

Not all complexities need to be untangled, but I think this one does. *Picnomon* is the genus and it's a genus with a sole representative, the soldier thistle. In biology-speak, genera with only one species are called monotypic.

It's a one-off, a solo, unaccompanied. No near relatives, no allies or alikes. A Robinson Crusoe of a plant.

*

Martha. Benjamin. George. Is this an overly associative way of thinking – maybe? – but the solitary soldier thistle takes me in a pretty straight line to those last-of-their-kind creatures. Those haunting, unutterably sad images of animals for whom there is no mate, no like mind or mirror image. The final curtain before zero.

Martha, the last passenger pigeon, died at Cincinnati Zoo in 1914.

Benjamin, the last thylacine (Tasmanian tiger) died at Hobart's Beaumaris Zoo in 1936.

George, the last-known Pinta Island tortoise, died at the Charles Darwin Research Station in the Galápagos in 2012.

The last quagga, an equine with zebra stripes on its front half, died in captivity in 1883.

I wonder about the loneliness experienced by Martha, Benjamin, George and the unnamed quagga as they paced or flew about their enclosures. Did their solitary status cause them some kind of instinctive malaise?

Of Benjamin there remains a handful of photographs and a minute's worth of monochrome footage.

The thylacine's final flicker.

There's a plot device known as deus ex machina. It originated in Greek and Roman theatre, and the literal translation is god from the machine. In practice it's where an impossible situation is resolved by the unexpected intervention of the gods or some other unlikely event. Euripides was particularly keen on the technique. Take *Orestes*. The play's penultimate page. Enter Apollo from above. Dropped in to tie up the loose ends.

In contemporary theatre (and film) the definition has frayed and expanded to describe any conclusion that defies the procedural logic of the storyline.

For Benjamin and all the other fauna and flora we've wiped from the face of the earth, there is no deus ex machina. Extinction is forever.

In *The Creation: An Appeal to Save Life on Earth*, evolutionary biologist Edward O. Wilson's manifesto-cum-elegy, he predicts an endgame of biological impoverishment. A world inhabited by *Homo sapiens*, domesticated animals, a small selection of crops and nothing else. 'What poets and scientists alike may choose to call the Eremozoic Era – the Age of Loneliness.'

Endlings. That's the noun invented to describe Martha, Benjamin, George and their ilk. Individuals that are the last of their species or subspecies. It's an obvious thing to say, but say it I shall. The fact that we need such a word does not reflect well on us and our stewardship of the planet.

The word 'endling' was suggested in a letter to the journal *Nature* in 1996. It provoked a spate of correspondence and several counter-suggestions, including relict, terminarch, yatim (Arabic for orphan) and ender, a term used by Chaucer in *The Canterbury Tales*.

*

I think the last melancholy word belongs to a parrot. A reminder that extinctions happen in the cultural sphere as well. In *The Descent of Man*, Darwin wrote that the explorer and naturalist Alexander von Humboldt 'saw in South America a parrot which was the sole living creature that could speak a word of the language of a lost tribe.' Humboldt took the bird back to Europe and phonetically transcribed its utterances. Those notes are the sole record of the vanished Atures language. Humboldt's own account of his travels mentions the parrot, but I wonder if the transcription story isn't apocryphal.

Paris. Early 1800s. *Amazona* encaged.
Souvenir. Survivor. Eye witness.
Keeper of other-speak.
Homesick for the bromeliads of the Orinoco.
And look – here's Humboldt in his armchair,
reading aloud,
(Voltaire – or maybe a review of the latest Molière)
coaxing syllables and vowel sounds
tick-tock bird gabble
unrequited parrot-talk.

A refugee washed up
in a foreign city where no one understands.

We live among close-connected shadows. A Murri
colleague once explained to me how his indigenous tongue
relied on the local vegetation for its figurative expression. If
a species of tree disappeared, so too would a metaphor from
their linguistic landscape.

*

Unlike the thylacine and the language of the Atures, the
soldier thistle is doing very nicely, thank you. Not endangered.
Nowhere close. A weed of minor scale.
Fizzled plants scoffing weeks of drought and storm.
Jaggy green melting into grey –
the colour of Jerusalem artichokes left to air.
Plants that stand for us
that stand also for themselves
as we stand for ourselves.

KILLING THISTLES

I

Killers. They're closer than you think. Think nearby shelf. Killer concentrate. Killer fast action. Killer ready to use. Natural weedkiller. In supermarket, garden centre and hardware store, oxymorons proliferate. By hook and hinge, along curtain tracks, contained promises of destruction. Death to thistle-heads. Bye-bye chickweed. Time's up for dandelion clocks. On packs and canisters, picket fences of capital letters and boldface DO NOTs. Do not apply if rain expected. Do not allow contact or drift. Imperative overkill. Keep your driveway nice. Keep out of reach.

*

Lightweight ladders and ceramic planters occupied the pavement, edged towards the post office next door. Seed packets promised bounties of carrots and petunias. The suburb's original post office is long gone from its graceful sandstone home. Relocated to a shopfront with all the charm and character of a crash barrier. My local hardware store was next door to it – until it closed down. Hardware stores are barometers of neighbourhood change, and I used to have this rule of thumb: when the hardware shuts up shop you know it's time to move. Sure there are dime stores and chains. But sometimes you want a reliable hammer and a sales assistant who knows his rivets. Hardware stores plug into DIY dramas of aspiration and salvage. Before mine closed for ever, I went for a last fix of its beeswax- and solvent-scented air – and checked out its selection of weedkillers. A few days later I walked down the aisle in one of those home supply barns. On its shelves was an array of killers to keep your garden free of bindii, docks and those all too common sow thistles. The domestic industry may have cleaned up its act somewhat, gone to glysophate or less toxic compounds, but in the agricultural area, 2,4-D persists.

*

Herbicidal mania. Power-sprays fog the market. A squirt or a few to wipe out weeds common or garden. Shoots to kill. Their roots undermine the dream. From farm to field to frontyard lawn, they befoul the place. Seeds waft through streets and suburbs as we sleep. Packs go overboard with warnings. Skulls and crossbones. Once were pirate flags, now flag poison. Keep containers closed tight, check regularly for leaks. Keep away. The weeds will overrun us, violate our beds, unless we get them first.

II

Scientific narratives rarely have a single beginning, but for convenience's sake, let's start here:

'Theologians have always held that man would not return to the Garden of Eden until he had achieved the state of grace befitting God's paradise. But today the chemist holds forth the prospect of a return to a possible state of Eden...'

Science, Servant of Man by Bernard Cohen, 1948.

The (chemical) war on weeds fired up as World War II drew to a close. In a tale of scientific happenstance 2,4-D and the related MCPA were discovered about the same time by researchers in the USA and Britain. By-products of military-sponsored studies into biological weaponry.

2,4-D is strong stuff. A synthesis of hard-to-pronounce ingredients. It's what's called a plant growth regulator. It mimics the natural hormone auxin, causing rapid cell growth, which blocks and eventually destroys the plant's vascular transport system. What distinguished 2,4-D was its selective character: the herbicide could suppress broadleaf plants (didcots) while leaving monocots like wheat, rice and other cereals unaffected.

The chronology of 2,4-D's journey from lab to literature to supply store shelf is complex, sometimes contested. In the beginning, the focus was using low doses to stimulate plant growth, but the vision splendid 'of wheat plants as large as bamboos, and cabbages beneath whose shade a regiment might shelter' proved fanciful. When they wrote up their results, researchers added a footnote that an overdose damaged or killed the plant. And before you could say megabucks, weed control was the endgame and rival companies were in court fighting over intellectual property rights.

Yet, even as litigation was in train, manufacturers were promoting their new weedkillers to an enthusiastic public.

'Science decrees death for lawn weeds', ran a 1946 headline in *The Pittsburgh Press*. 'The common thistle dies almost pronto. And it's all due to a miracle chemical formula… 2,4-D.'

The Central Queensland Herald announced with glee that in 1947, 'more than 95 per cent of the carrots marketed were sprayed with chemicals instead of being hand-weeded'.

Thank God for biochemistry! was the refrain. Weed control would no more be a hit-and-miss affair involving corrosive materials or back-breaking toil. The ploughman would no longer plod his weary way home as he did in Thomas Gray's 1751 elegy. He'd clock off with a straight back and energy aplenty for evening classes or ball games with the kids. Weekends he'd buy products with brand names like Weed-A-Bomb, and join forces with fellow warriors defending their turf from the evil of sow thistles and clover.

But the story doesn't snap neatly shut. Come 2015 the thistles are back. Resistance to 2,4-D confirmed in three populations of South Australian sow thistles.

*

Plants growing themselves to death was a recurring theme long before 2,4-D arrived on the scene. In a prolix opinion piece in the *Adelaide Observer* of May 1868, the anonymous writer suggests the most efficient way of controlling thistles may be to 'let the land purge itself by becoming thistle-sick, surfeited with the one product'.

This idea isn't quite as science fiction as it sounds.

In the last quarter of the nineteenth century, various experiments were conducted. Their purpose: to find reliable and economical methods to reduce thistle loads on agricultural land. One of the most widely reported was from regional Victoria, where the perennial creeping thistle was running riot. Without going into the technicalities of this trial, it was a bit like fast-forwarding the growth cycle. And then pressing the repeat button. The aim was to arrest maturity, once, twice, multiple times, and thereby weaken the plants – or to use the phrase then in circulation, exhaust them.

Compared to dousing fields with chemical gravies of uncertain legacy, this low-tech rotation of growth and ploughing makes good environmental sense.

*

I found it between Travel and Pets. *Weeds*, 1958. Cracked spine, minor foxing, the odd dog-ear – the used-book trade has a penchant for canines. Published by the New South Wales Department of Agriculture for the man on the land. To dear Terry, in sloping blue ink on the title page. Happy Christmas, love from Aunty Pam. *Weeds*, a present from the past. Was Terry a young farmer starting out? His life brought momentarily back from oblivion. In the future, in a shop like this, will someone open a book and see my name in the top right-hand corner?

Lifetimes of reading unspool. Hardbacks loose with age, piles of paperback crime and romance. And always the prospect of fortuitous discovery. In secondhand bookshops you find things you didn't know you wanted – like *Weeds*. Faded at the seams. A staining of insects who ate their way through the words on pages 86–87. The text is only part of the story with pre-owned books. There's also the miscellany between their leaves: shopping lists, a recipe for coffee cake or an obituary snipped from the newspaper, a moth wing, a letter if you're lucky. This was Terry's handbook. Do those spots of candle wax on the cover speak of power cuts? Unpaid bills? The shape of a family farm fallen on hard times?

Once upon a time there was another Terry. A primary school classmate with witchy hands and hair the colour of molasses. She was hit by a car while crossing the road and killed. Death had been a remote concept, confined to war and the world of grown-ups. Terry's accident brought it home. Things could go wrong that couldn't be repaired. A few months after the crash I ran into Mrs Terry – I don't remember their surname – at the local library. Talking non-stop, talking nonsense. Barking mad. I was seven or eight, I didn't understand the longevity of grief. Or the way it might unhinge a mother who'd lost her only child.

In the paddock, thistles unlock their flower buds. Host honeybees and Lepidoptera. 'Don't argue with weeds – kill them with Nocweed.' Among my collection of technical literature gleaned from garage sales and charity shops I've got another state government publication: *Weed Control with Chemicals*, circa 1956. Full of diagrams and charts, fuzzy black and white photos and ads for yesterday's killers. But no handwritten inscription to kindle the imagination.

*

It's the early 1990s and thanks to a Performing Arts Scholarship I've spent the last couple of months studying Vietnamese theatre in Hanoi. Now I'm on the train heading south to the city everyone still calls Saigon. Night falls – suddenly, as it does in this latitude. Outside the window settlements flash into view, then loose themselves in a dark nowhere that swallows up the past. Dawn breaks just after Da Nang. When I open the jalousie to see where we are, I'm greeted by a scene of devastation. Burnt. Brown. Blighted. A wasteland of stumps and withered vegetation. Like those photographs of World War I you see in every school history book and every year in the lead-up to Anzac Day. As if those images of Passchendaele and the Somme have been projected onto the windows of this Vietnamese train. It shocks me to see barely a trace of green where once were croplands and rainforest. But even more disturbing is the silence. The train has stopped and I push down the window. Not a sound. No animals foraging for food, no birdsong, not a scratch, not a purr of life in that former forest, now quiet like death itself.

You can't write about 2,4-D without mentioning Vietnam. The compound was one of two active ingredients in the notorious Agent Orange, the defoliant used by the American armed forces in Vietnam. The other ingredient was 2,4,5-T, which carried most of the dioxin contamination.

In his inaugural address John F. Kennedy called on the United States, its allies and adversaries, 'to invoke the wonders of science instead of its terrors'. Eleven months later he sanctioned the use of defoliants in a secret operation code-named Ranch Hand. Yet, even as the administration was debating the use of these chemicals in Southeast Asia, questions about their safety and spread remained unanswered. Enter Rachel Carson and *Silent Spring*. Her 1962 book was not only an environmental wake-up call, but also a critique of what was then current thinking about scientific progress and the subjugation of nature. 'The chemical weed killers are a bright new toy', said Carson. Predictably, the manufacturing giants closed ranks and threatened legal action.

In the central cordillera and the Mekong delta, planes circled overhead. A fine yellow mist descended. The next day leaves wilted. Within a week the terrain was bald. When the war ended in 1975 about ten per cent of Vietnam had been drenched in millions of litres of toxic herbicides. But it's the human stories, not the statistics, that make the point.

Half an hour later, the train starts moving again. I close the window but the view through the glass doesn't alter. It rolls on, mile after mile. A bleak, blank, denuded landscape. War on a people is equally war on the biodiversity that sustains them. We tend to forget or overlook that aspect. Remnants of trees recall what has been lost – and what persists. Residues of Agent Orange remain in the ecosystem, have settled in the soil and seeped into the water supply. If you lived here you'd be familiar with it, perhaps you'd feel it in the roots of your teeth and in your lymph nodes. In your cochleae and all the other Latin bits and pieces of yourself.

The story of 2,4-D involves leaps. From improving plant growth to killing weeds. From agriculture to weapon of mass defoliation – payback for the military's investment in the early development and testing of 2,4-D.

After the war, the US poured rivers of cash into chasing ghosts – trying to locate servicemen believed missing in action in Indochina. What a shame there wasn't the same zeal for remediation and humanitarian aid to help the Vietnamese deal with the fallout of Agent Orange. Because, as Rachel Carson warned decades ago, 'Chemical war is never won, and all life is caught in its violent crossfire.'

III

'Every one should destroy a thistle whenever he has an opportunity', declared the *Sydney Morning Herald* in 1849. 'There is a time for everything under the sun, and now is the time for the extirpation of thistles', wrote a correspondent to the *Argus* ten years later. Referring to the Old Testament's Ecclesiastes: 'To every thing there is a season, and a time to every purpose…a time to plant, and a time to pluck up that which is planted…a time to kill'.

To research thistles is to read a lot about killing. Regular verbs like destroy, abolish, eradicate, erase, annihilate, obliterate, exterminate – and one I hadn't encountered until I started reading about thistles: extirpate. The word is widespread in archives. Nineteenth-century landowners and lawmakers agitated for the extirpation of thistles: 'The spread of the thistles is an evil that must no longer be overlooked.'

Proclamations with a Biblical ring.

Uttered from that place where common sense prevails and things stand to reason.

Or not.

They would extirpate, they have extirpated.

To extirpate means to root out and destroy completely. Extinction wipes a species from the face of the earth; extirpation removes it from a given region or locality. First used around 1530, extirpation derives from the Latin *exstirpare*, *ex* meaning out, and *stirps* meaning a stem or trunk. It's a noun that harks back. To gentlemen in frock coats, imperial gusto and lines drawn with rulers. It implies violence, the elimination of thistlekind.

'Every farmer in the colony is interested in the extirpation of this troublesome weed.'

The Adelaide Observer, November 1854.

A weed is the opposite of being a tourist because it's at home wherever it lands. *Cirsium* or *Carduus diaspora*. They came in clod and sod with empire. Followed inroads made by spade and plough. Planned by no one, thistles flower along the edge, dustmops of purple that clasp the light. A lyrical sacrilege. Later come seeds full of purpose. Brush them with a boot or a skirt hem and they're instant migrants, off in search of new ground. Leaving behind skeleton stalks that conjure dark medieval mysteries. Tough and bristly, thistles are outsiders, rocking up on frontier land, putting down roots and sending up buds which once upon a harder time than now were cooked and eaten. Gatecrashers and flora non grata most, but the odd species jumped the fence to join the ergasiophygophytes – a gang of botanical escapees. The word 'ergasiophygophyte' was devised by Swiss botanists in the early twentieth century. Along with a heap of other polysyllabic terms cobbled together from Greek stems and prefixes. To make the business of classifying alien species more scientific – or at least sound more scientific than weeding out or extirpation.

IV

In 1947 the Dow Chemical Company released *Death to Weeds*, a 16 mm film championing its latest product: 2,4-D. 'One of the newest and most versatile weapons in Dow's arsenal of chemical warfare', explained the off-screen Voice of Authority. What follows is a twenty-minute hallelujah to the brave, new, weed-free world promised by 2,4-D.

Films like *Death to Weeds* go by several names – sponsored, promotional, corporate – but my favourite descriptor is ephemeral. Ephemeral films were made for advertising, educational, training, even propaganda purposes. Any focus on cinematic art was (usually) incidental. Commissioned by private firms, community groups, governments and other public agencies, their heyday was the middle of the last century, and they documented not so much the reality of the time, but rather the wishful thinking of the time. Suburban life though a rose-tinted lens. Faith in science and technology to see us right.

Death to Weeds was aimed at the agricultural and industrial sectors, but manufacturers also ran campaigns to sell their weedkillers into the postwar domestic market. Weeds are our common foe, the film's invisible narrator reminds us, and whether you're 'a home owner with a lawn and garden to maintain, [or] a greens-keeper at a golf club… Dow agricultural chemists have the answer'.

*

Once produced in huge numbers, for a long time ephemeral films languished in the dusty margins of media history. Although many are now available in archives and on YouTube, many have been lost or survive only as fragments. To help fill that gap, here's my ephemeral film script for Whatever Brand Weedkiller, circa – let's say 1953.

EXT. SUBURBAN GARDEN – DAY.

A summer's day. A front garden. At first glance it appears well maintained, but on closer inspection we see that it's being choked by weeds. A chaos of ragwort, plantain and dwarf thistles.

Insects buzz around the thistles' purple flowers.

JOAN, an immaculately made-up housewife in her late twenties, is on her hands and knees pulling out weeds.

She tries to remove a particularly recalcitrant specimen. The plant doesn't budge but JOAN breaks a fingernail. She looks at the damage to her manicure and sighs.

> MALE AUTHORITY (V.O.)
> The story of the MacFarlane garden was not a happy one. Mrs MacFarlane has spent more hours than she cares to count on her hands and knees.

EXT. SUBURBAN GARDEN – EARLY EVENING.

Later the same day. The same front garden choked with weeds. The sun hangs low in the sky, the shadows are long.

PHIL, a middle-manager in his middle-thirties, rolls up his sleeves. Picks up a hoe.

> MALE AUTHORITY (V.O.)
> Summer evenings after he gets home from the office, Mr MacFarlane takes his turn.

He attempts to dig up a patch of well-established weeds. It's hard going and he soon works up quite a sweat.

JOAN comes out with a tray of refreshments. She pours a glass of cold beer and hands it to PHIL.

> PHIL
> I don't know Joan, despite our best efforts those pesky weeds keep coming.

> JOAN
> (sighing)
> We've got the worst-looking lawn on the block.

> PHIL
> (also sighing)
> We sure have.

> JOAN
> And it's terribly embarrassing, Phil. I'm afraid to show my face in church. And I'm sure that's why the Battersbys didn't invite us to their last barbeque.

INT. BEDROOM – NIGHT.

Moonlight streams into the room through a gap in the curtains.

In their twin beds, JOAN and PHIL toss and turn. Plagued by nightmares of monstrous weeds.

Fade up classic horror-movie music. A wavering Theremin,

or perhaps a few dissonant, unsettling chord clusters.

DISSOLVE TO:

EXT. SUBURBAN GARDEN – NIGHT.

In the shimmering semi-dark, a plot of weeds takes on a sinister appearance.

Fade up sounds of botanic activity. Seeds cracking, leaves rustling, stems snapping.

Time-lapse. A new thistle sprouts, forms a rosette, grows into a full-size plant. Keeps on growing. And growing.

Other weeds do likewise. Until the plot is full of writhing, out-of-control plants.

INT. BEDROOM – NIGHT.

The classic horror-movie music returns.

JOAN awakes from her nightmare with a strangled gasp. Sits bolt upright in bed. Breathing heavily.

EXT. SUBURBAN GARDEN – EARLY EVENING.

It's a new day. A happy, smartly dressed JOAN stands on the lawn in high heels. Watering can in hand. Daintily killing weeds.

PHIL arrives home carrying a large container of Whatever Brand Weedkiller.

> PHIL
> Look what I bought today. Whatever Brand Weedkiller. A safe and convenient solution to our problem.

JOAN bursts out laughing.

> MALE AUTHORITY (V.O.)
> The joke is that on her shopping jaunt that same afternoon Mrs MacFarlane also bought a can of Whatever Brand Weedkiller.

> JOAN
> It's economical, too. A marvel of modern science.

> PHIL
> The workless way to a weed-free garden.

PHIL and JOAN smile to camera. Who wouldn't want to be Mr and Mrs Perfect? And all it takes is a purchase of Whatever Brand Weedkiller.

> MALE AUTHORITY (V.O.)
> Don't let thousands of soil-grasping leafy weeds smother your lawn or borders! Don't waste time mixing costly preparations that don't kill roots and all. Get Whatever Brand Weedkiller, and sleep peacefully at night.

INT. BEDROOM – NIGHT.

Moonlight streams into the room through a gap in the curtains.

JOAN and PHIL are both fast asleep in their twin beds.

DISSOLVE TO:

EXT. SUBURBAN GARDEN – PRE-DAWN.

The same plot of weeds as before.

Time-lapse. The full-grown plants wilt, drop their leaves, shrink to almost nothing.

A large container of Whatever Brand Weedkiller is placed beside the dead weeds.

Fade up music. Something pastoral and vaguely familiar like the fifth movement of Beethoven's Sixth Symphony.

The sun rises. Whatever Brand Weedkiller is bathed in golden light.

MALE AUTHORITY (V.O.)
Whatever Brand Weedkiller. Buy it now! Apply it now!

AFGHAN & OTHER NATIVE THISTLES

I

The Afghan thistle is neither a thistle nor from Afghanistan. It's not even part of the Asteraceae family, where true thistles belong. Botanically speaking, *Solanum hoplopetalum* is a member of the *Solonaceae* or nightshades, which means it's more closely related to tomatoes and potatoes than it is to thistles.

Calling it a thistle reflects our tendency to label any prickly plant a thistle.

Thistle by name.

Thistle by nature – or maybe not.

Because my interest lies in the cultural life of thistles and those plants we dub thistles, I'm including the Afghan thistle in my extended family of – what shall I call them? Socially defined thistles.

But first a bit more botany.

Solanum hoplopetalum is endemic to Western Australia. There's a kindred South Australian plant, *Solanum hystrix*, and for a while it was assumed the two were one and the same species. They're not, but their many similarities do suggest a common ancestry.

While *S. hystrix* is virtually glabrous – that's the technical term for leaves or stems devoid of hairs – Afghan thistles are hirsute, bristly, super-prickly. Three of its four popular names reference this quality:

Thorny solanum.

Porcupine solanum.

Prickly potato weed.

Afghan thistle behaves like a weed. One of the few natives deemed noxious in its home state, it's been declared a pest plant in a number of shires. And it regularly pops up on watchlists.

A public nuisance. A miscreant.

'It is very troublesome in cultivated land…Prompt action is necessary when Afghan thistle makes its appearance.'

Western Mail, Perth, January 1932.

Here's a sketch compiled from eyewitness accounts:

Afghan thistle is a sprawling perennial, a literal low-life – it seldom exceeds twenty centimetres in height. Leaves are lobed and covered with long, straw-coloured spines. Flowers are star-shaped, have yellow centres and petals that go from palest blue to moonlight. Berries are black, or maybe greenish-yellow – descriptions are inconsistent.

S. hoplopetalum forms colonies, and plants which on the surface appear separate are actually joined together by horizontal, below-ground stems. Although it produces seeds, reproduction is primarily by vegetative means; i.e., reshooting from those underground stems each spring. Or following a bushfire.

'Appearing first, a number of years ago, in our arid goldfields area around Kalgoorlie, it has now spread eastward into the wheat belt, where it has become a very common weed in waste places, on fallow land, and wherever the soil carries sufficient moisture in the summer.'

Communication from Mr W. M. Carne of the WA Department of Agriculture, quoted in *A New Solanum from Western Australia* by G. Bitter & V. S. Summerhayes, 1926.

After a breathless stretch of sunshine and hot weather,

epic cloudscapes presage a storm…
when it comes
thunder and lightning firework the sky
but any rain evaporates in the air
and all the trails run dry.
Here the thistles' pointed intensity is found
on the shoulders
of roads and dirt tracks.
Expanding along transport corridors.
In cultivated fields and open woodlands.
On scarp breakaways and excavations.
In civic margins,
frayed corners of corporate landscaping,
on rail embankments and unvisited patches of scrub,
the Afghan thistles are flowering.

*

Single words yield vast social histories. *Solanum hoplopetal-um*'s popular name alludes to the belief that it was spread beyond its native range by Afghan camel herders. This may or may not be true, but a kind of folk botany has grown around the notion.

By the mid-1800s the push was on to claim the interior of the continent. Imaginatively as well as physically.

Prospectors, pastoralists, pioneers.

Inland exploration required pack animals able to stay the course and handlers to manage those animals. June 1860, twenty-four camels and three handlers disembarked at Port Melbourne. More soon followed. As the century unrolled these cameleers and their 'ships of the desert' carted supplies, delivered mail, and took part in scientific expeditions.

The recruited cameleers were young or middle-aged

men on two- or three-year contracts. And they arrived alone, forbidden from bringing their wives and families to Australia. They came from Afghanistan, from neighbouring regions (Kashmir, India, Pakistan), from Persia, Egypt and Turkey. Their loyalties and heritages were diverse but they were united by an Islamic faith – and being lumped together as 'Afghans' by a white Australia blind to, and uninterested in, their cultural differences.

The majority of Australians knew little about Afghanistan. A thorn in the flank of imperial ambition, a country fighting a suite of wars against British control. The place where Dr Watson received wounds to his shoulder and subclavian artery, and contracted enteric (typhoid) fever.

'"Dr Watson, Mr Sherlock Holmes," said Stamford, introducing us.

"How are you?" he said cordially, gripping my hand with a strength for which I should hardly have given him credit. "You have been in Afghanistan, I perceive."

"How on earth did you know that?" I asked in astonishment.'

A Study in Scarlet by Arthur Conan Doyle, 1887.

Or perhaps they leafed through Lady Florentia Sale's account of the retreat from Kabul? The major-general's wife put the wind up Victorian readers with her unflinching narrative. *A Journal of the Disasters in Afghanistan, 1841–2* travels from memsahib life in the Kabul cantonments where 'the cauliflowers, artichokes, and turnip radishes are very fine' to frostbite, hunger and roads 'covered with awfully mangled bodies'.

Nineteenth-century Afghanistan was poor, but it was a strategic gateway for a Russian attack on British India. Hence:

The First Anglo-Afghan War.
The Second Anglo-Afghan War.
The Third Anglo-Afghan War.

II

In Australia the cameleers were assigned living quarters on the outskirts of settlements which became known as Ghantowns.

Shanties of canvas and corrugated iron; homemade mosques and vegetable plots. Fences that stood out against cyanic skies and sandy soils.

The desert became the recipient of unheard songs and voices.

As the outback communities became more established, many camel drivers set up their own businesses. Such moves led to resentment – not always, but often. And in some places, open hostility. Afghans were mocked and maligned in public discourse; racist episodes were routine; magazine articles, newspaper columns, letters to the editor and popular fiction revelled in horror stories of miscegenation.

'Yadoo Mahomet Kurda was young, tall, robust. He had black hair, a black beard, and great sleepy black eyes, which when they rested on the face of a woman, could leap into fire and blaze like quartz crystals on a hot day.'

That's from the 1908 short story 'A Coolgardie idyll' by A. G. Hales.

A couple of pages later:

'The Afghan lolled on his low couch and watched Mrs Jepson under his thick, heavy, eyelids; she sat and worked embroidery, and knew nothing.'

No prizes for guessing where that story ends up.

Then there was The Case of Miss Wolseley, or The Domestic Servant and The Afghan. This convoluted tale of an English immigrant and her romantic relationship with a man called either Ameer Mahomet or Ameer Khan, who was either a hawker or a horse dealer, was picked up (and sensationalised) by the press. A Perth newspaper took credit for its pivotal role in the drama. It had 'saved her, practically against her will, possibly from a fate worse than death. As a matter of fact, it was only after learning through *The Sunday Times* that Elizabeth was again in communication with her dusky admirer that the Government decided to send her home'.

The Sunday Times, Perth, January 1911.

Women were the weak link in the white Australia line.

On the Western Australian goldfields these tensions reached flashpoint.

Today Coolgardie markets itself to tourists as a mining ghost town, but in 1898 it boasted a parade of shops, hotels, banks, breweries, a mosque, a synagogue, several churches, seven newspapers, a racecourse and two theatres. It was also home to the largest Muslim community in the colony.

When alluvial gold was discovered in 1892 it made headlines around the world. Fortune seekers rushed to Coolgardie; t'othersiders from across the Nullarbor were joined by speculators and dreamers from North America, Africa, Europe, the British Isles, New Zealand and elsewhere.

All looking for a better life.

'[All] prepared to migrate hither as soon as the reports were confirmed, and it was proved that the wealth of the somnolent and dreary interior was not concentrated in a few acres.'

History of Western Australia by Warren Bert Kimberly, 1897.

III

Such was Coolgardie's fame that 'a play in five acts', *The Duchess of Coolgardie*, was produced in London's West End in 1896, and at Sydney's Criterion Theatre two years later. As a playwright this piqued my interest, of course it did, so I tracked down the script by Euston Leigh and Cyril Clare.

'Never before has Australian mining life been so marvellously and realistically reproduced on the stage', enthused a London correspondent for the *Newcastle Morning Herald and Miners' Advocate*.

The *Age* disagreed: 'Sheer drivel from beginning to end.'

The play is a potluck of melodrama enlivened with Australian colour and setting. On the subject of which, the co-writers were obviously unfamiliar with the geography of the Coolgardie area.

'Act 1 Scene 2.

The wilderness. This scene, which occupies the whole stage, should indicate the wild shrub, dense foliage of the eucalypti and indigenous gum trees of the Australian regions...The graduation of light conveys the impression that the day is breaking in the forest...'

A bit further into the scene:

'SYBIL. What a lovely spot! A perfect garden of ferns and flowers.'

Over the page there's a moss-covered stump which turns out to be 'a monster nugget of gold'.

Forest, ferns, moss...About the only physical feature the script does get right is the constant lack of water.

The characters have names like Myles Hooligan and Bendigo Bill, and the dialogue is written in a range of Irish, Scottish and English regional accents. There's an Aboriginal character called Wallaroo who sounds as if he's wandered in from the Mississippi delta, and who was, for some inexplicable reason, played by a female actor in the London production.

There are fisticuffs and farce aplenty, detailed stage directions, and almost every speech is prefaced with information about its delivery: angrily, defiantly, overwhelmed, surprised, bewildered and horror-stricken, etc. When I write dialogue I may indicate if I want a line to be whispered or sung, but other than that, I prefer collaborators to make their own discoveries. And besides, actor friends have told me that one of the first things they do when they start rehearsal is cross out those adverbs and instructions.

Fashions in performance writing change.

Like most plays of its era, *The Duchess of Coolgardie* gives comprehensive explanations of costumes, props, lighting and sets – which I find more interesting than the overwrought drama.

Somewhere in theatre's history this prose and padding got added. Read a play by Shakespeare and his stage directions are basic:

'Exit, pursued by a bear.' *The Winter's Tale*.

Or delve into the candlelit and treacherous universe of the Jacobeans:

'Enter Vindice, with the skull of his love dressed up in tires [elaborate headwear].' *The Revenger's Tragedy*.

Modern playwrights have gone back to the essentials, and these days it's not uncommon to find scripts with no movement text and minimal scene descriptions. Mine go like this:

'A bar. A small neon palm tree.' *Songket*.

Actually, there wasn't a single *Duchess of Coolgardie*; there were several shows by that name, or versions thereof, touring Australia and New Zealand in the late 1890s. As well as the London original, there was another *The Duchess of Coolgardie*, sometimes called *The Little Duchess of Coolgardie* and *The Queen of Coolgardie*. The storylines and casts of these similarly titled productions were different – but not that different.

'It is interesting to learn by last mail that the script of the Drury Lane drama *The Duchess of Coolgardie* has not yet been sent out to Mr Bland Holt, the purchaser of the Australian rights of the play. Yet it is not long since a certain author-actor-manager played in parts of this colony a drama of the same name and announced it as the latest London success. Mr. George Darrell too, if I remember right, announced his play, *The Queen of Coolgardie*, as the "great Drury Lane drama".'

Evening Post, Wellington, New Zealand, April 1897.

There's also the mystery of the playwright or playwrights plural.

'All sorts of rumours as to the authorship of the piece are current.'

The Star, Christchurch, New Zealand, November 1896.

The credited writers are Euston Leigh and Cyril Clare, but after some archival trawling, I'm pretty certain they're pseudonyms. Stage gossip suggested that John Coleman, the producer of the London show, was one or both of the co-writers.

The Star again, a fortnight later: 'He [Coleman] has consequently grafted on local colour *ad lib.*, assisted by Mr Julius Price, Lord Fingall, Mr Marriott-Watson and others.'

The *New York Times* ventured a somewhat tongue-in-cheek alternative: *The Duchess of Coolgardie* 'was written by Euston Leigh and Cyril Clare, otherwise Mr Barney Barnato, the Kafir King, and Mr Haddon Chambers'.

Barnato was a financier and diamond magnate, but Haddon Chambers was a dramatist, a prolific one with West End and Broadway hits on his CV. Moreover, the gentleman-turned-adventurer (à la Big Ben in *The Duchess of Coolgardie*) was a recurring character in his plays, likewise the hardships of outback Australia. In the last decade of the nineteenth century he wrote a number of plays with partners...so it is just possible that these lines came from his pen:

'*(Bell of Camel Team heard outside.)*
GLEN. Hello! Do you hear that? The Camel Team's in! Water, lads.'

IV

At an open-air meeting in Coolgardie's Bayley Street on the evening of Saturday 22 December 1894 the editor of the *Coolgardie Miner*, Frederick Vosper, addressed the assembled crowd. His speech reiterated the sentiments of an article he'd written for his newspaper four days previously. A vitriolic opinion piece full of rhetorical questions and exclamation marks, a call to action to defend the white man's Australia from 'undesirable immigrants'. The outcome of the December meeting was the foundation of the Anti-Asiatic League.

The Afghan residents who were the subject of Vosper's ire were in an invidious position. He railed against their entrepreneurial success. Their ownership of 'shops, and stores, and plots of ground, chains of footpaths, and probably banks as well'. He likened them to fever and drought. Even the Afghans' temperance vexed him:

'In the very virtues of these dusky exiles lies the greatest fear: they are abstemious, especially as regards alcoholic liquors, and this means the saving of money.'

Others shared Vosper's sentiments.

'Owing to the action of "alien" shop-keepers at Fremantle in keeping their stores open till long after 6 o'clock at night, the shop assistants at the port are fearful that the breaches of the early closing custom will spread to a serious extent, meaning longer hours of labour for them. In order to discuss the situation a largely-attended meeting of shop assistants was held…The circular convening the meeting declared that…[The offenders] were "in every instance Jews, Chinamen, and Afghans".'

The West Australian, January 1897.

*

England, the mid-1970s. For a so-called nation of shopkeepers the situation was paradoxical. In suburban Hertfordshire, our nearby shops shut five o'clock on the dot. One afternoon a week was early closing – to compensate for opening Saturday morning – and Sundays were a retail desert. Until migrants from the subcontinent came along, took stock, and thought they could do better. Which they did. Much better.

Later, as a second- and third-year undergraduate I lived on Oxford's Walton Street. In our immediate vicinity was a newsagent, an off-licence (bottle shop) and a grocery-cum-general store run by a family from Bangladesh. It was where we went when we ran out of milk; when we got dope-induced cravings for chocolate digestives or halva at 9.00 pm; where I discovered fresh coriander and lime pickle so hot, hot, hot it practically blasted you into orbit.

One cold, soggy evening I dashed in to buy a samosa. The shop was empty but for the proprietor – I think his name was Mr Datta – gazing out the window at the rain-blurred light across the street. He stood there not moving while I waited to be served. He may have been silently cursing the weather that was keeping his customers indoors, but I imagined him remembering the monsoons of Dhaka or Rangpur. I imagined him looking back into the past. Which is also another country.

The other side of this brave new world of shopkeeping was brought home to me a few years afterwards by a community theatre colleague. Her father worked eighteen hours, seven days a week in a corner store, every day except Christmas, to make things easier for his children. Easier than they'd been for him, arriving at Heathrow Airport with his worldly goods packed in a biscuit tin.

*

193

Back in Coolgardie.

Vosper was by no means the only xenophobe in town, but he was one of the most vocal. Because I pictured him a booze-bloated, red-faced bloke around the age of fifty, I was taken aback to see a photograph of a slender, rather bohemian-looking man with long black hair. A radical, a republican – and a racist. He died young, at the age of thirty-one. That makes Vosper just twenty-five when he wrote: 'These men [Afghans] are nothing to us. They are not of our creeds – our race. They menace our progress, our liberty, and our very right to live.' He called for 'total disqualification to these people of any employment under our Municipal Government…the stoppage of these Asiatic importations, and the deporting of those now here.'

Where on earth did all that rage and hatred come from?

*

The lot of the Afghan migrant in nineteenth-century Australia was not a happy one. They were scapegoats, blamed for myriad ills:

Undercutting wages.

Polluting waterholes.

Spreading weeds.

There were occasional expressions of appreciation and welcome – Aboriginal communities were more kindly disposed to the newcomers – but positive stories are thin on the ground. The voices of the cameleers themselves were barely documented. Their legacy rests in the memories of descendants, in collections of artefacts and visual records held by museums.

To find a more sympathetic treatment of Afghan migrants from that period I had to go to Calcutta. To *Kabuliwala* by Bengali writer Rabindranath Tagore. A bitter sweet tale of friendship between a dried-fruit seller from Kabul and the author's young daughter, who reminds the merchant of his own child back home.

V

I can't discuss the camel drivers of Western Australia without mentioning the sad case of Jumna Khan.

'Afghan runs amok with axe.'

The West Australian, December 1896.

'Murders one man with an axe. Chops another down.'

Daily News, Perth, December 1896.

Three months later a jury of twelve white men took just eight minutes to decide their verdict.

Court Official: Gentlemen of the jury, do you find the prisoner guilty or not guilty?

The Foreman: Guilty.

His Honour (to the Prisoner): Have you anything to say before sentence is passed upon you?

The Prisoner (through the Interpreter): I am very ill. My heart is affected. I leave myself in the hands of the court. Do what you please.

Justice Edward Stone put on the black cap and pronounced sentence.

The facts of the crime were not in dispute. Around midday on Thursday 3 December, Jumna Khan killed one man and injured another. Both victims were unknown to Khan, the attacks unprovoked. Newspapers reported the incident in detail, initially portraying the Afghan as 'a madman, or something next door thereto'.

'An insane Afghan' ran a headline in the *Inquirer and Commercial News*.

In the *West Australian* the 'fury of a maniac' was accompanied by 'shouting out in unintelligible language'.

Most reports mentioned that in the lead-up to the incident Jumna Khan's behaviour was somewhat eccentric.

He wandered about Fremantle for at least two days before the assault. He sought accommodation without success, until a police constable took him to the Victoria Coffee Palace and negotiated a makeshift bed in an outhouse. Khan waited in the sitting room, but when told his sleepout was ready he refused to move, clinging to a table leg. Eventually he left, barefoot, by way of the window, scrambled over the back wall and disappeared into the night. He probably slept at the rail yard. At the Railway Office the next morning he tried to purchase a ticket to Calcutta. He wandered around town some more. He entered a draper's, complained of fatigue, and tried to explain to the manager that he'd been robbed of £7. By all accounts he was distressed. He attempted to buy a revolver…

At his trial, Khan's Coolgardie manager, Mohammed Ameer, gave the following testimony – recorded in Judge Stone's Notes of Evidence:

'He has been in Colony about two years and worked for Faiz and Tagh Mahomet…Remember prisoner being sent to Menzies. He went with a camel team. I saw him after in Coolgardie. He came back by himself and an Englishman. I gave the Englishman £2 for bringing the prisoner to the camp…When prisoner returned to camp with the Englishman he would not speak to anyone but sat away by himself. Was very bad tempered. Would not do any work. He said he was very frightened someone wanted to shoot him and he wanted to go home…I took him to the police sergeant and told him. Also took his revolver from him as he was dangerous. The police sergeant said I had better pay him and let him go…I paid prisoner £42-8-0. I took him to the Coolgardie Railway Station. A ticket was taken for him to Boorabbin and then Albany…Prisoner was liked by his countrymen. He was a quiet man – never fight with anyone – no one complained to me about him.'

The Englishman was never named. As far as I can tell, no one tried to find out who he was. Or investigate his role – if any – in the subsequent tragedy.

Gilbert Probyn Smith, journalist and 'interpreter of the Oriental tongues', did more than translate proceedings for Jumna Khan. He confirmed the accused was terrified that someone was out to kill him, but dismissed his fear as foolish. And he took it upon himself to speculate not only about the psychology of the individual prisoner, whose 'brain was heated by continency, consequent upon being so long in the bush', but about his countrymen en masse: 'There is an expression that an Afghan goes "must" that is he has no control over himself at times.'

The interpreter for the Crown also weighed in with his opinion of Jumna Khan: 'He is a very illiterate Indian. I had difficulty in getting answers from him. He went from one subject to another.'

Khan's lawyer was pleading his client's insanity. To counter medical evidence given by the prosecution, he called one Owen Frank Paget, 'a legally qualified medical practitioner residing at Fremantle'. Paget's diagnosis was 'delusional insanity'. Symptoms: 'Incoherent replies, childish conduct' and running down the corridor listening to imaginary sounds.

The court transcripts are utterly pedestrian collections of words. And utterly heartbreaking.

Today it seems obvious that Jumna Khan was suffering from a mental illness. Today we know that psychosis doesn't appear out of the blue; there are usually warning signs, months, even years beforehand.

But in 1897 psychiatry as a profession barely existed.

And the jury didn't buy it. They found Reg. No. 18508 Jumna Khan guilty of wilful murder.

The press which had initially branded him a madman and a maniac now circulated a different narrative.

'Imbued with the idea that he had been robbed and insulted by a European, he gave vent to his pent-up feelings of bitter hatred against the white race by running amok in High-street, Fremantle.'

The West Australian, March 1897.

While back in Coolgardie, Vosper sprayed his customary venom.

'The sane and sensible alien is not a desirable colonist, and when he gets "off his Afghan chump," and starts in to thin out the all conquering white, he is entitled to no other consideration than that which the hangman may be disposed to show him.'

Coolgardie Miner, March 1897.

A Petition for Remission of Sentence was filed by Khan's solicitor. To His Excellency – with all the pomp and puffery of empire. At the end, a mere twenty signatures.

The Governor replied.

'This case has been fully and carefully considered in Executive Council, and that I am informed by Ministers that the Petition before me contains no fresh or additional grounds upon which they can advise me that Pardon or Reprieve should take place.

'The sentence pronounced by Law will therefore be carried out.'

Jumna Khan was hanged by the neck at the behest of strangers, among strangers, far from his native land. He declined the services of Mullah Mirza Khan and spent his final hours in prayer with fellow prisoner Azzam Khan, to whom he confided a few biographical details.

He was forty years old. Born in Afghanistan. Once upon a time he'd been married but his wife got involved with another man. He went after that man, failed to catch him, and killed his wife. He had two brothers living in Peshawar (then part of British India) and fled there with his daughter. He left the girl in Peshawar when he came to work in Western Australia.

VI

American historian Daniel Richter talks about layered pasts. A geology of different cultural seams where earlier strata remain beneath the surface to sculpt the contours of the present.

Traces of this particular substrata of Afghan migrant workers are visible not only inside museums and archives, but remain in surnames, in date palms and a large population of feral camels.

Check the nationalities of our early naturalists, glance at the adverts and story shards in nineteenth-century newspapers, and you soon realise that colonial Australia was a more diverse world than its popular Anglo-Celtic image conveys. A world of polyglot scientists, traders and cross-cultural relationships. A world in which, way before airlines, long-distance travel was a wholesale experience.

*

Afghan thistles are survivors. They survive agricultural activity and, thanks to their creeping habit and underground life, they survive herbicidal assault as well.

They line the margins and spangle pasture. Network of prickles and flowers white, so white they're almost blue.
Scenes sharp with a sense of strangeness
the drone of insectkind
air redolent of pilaf and cardamom
lush with mutton fat
bold from neglect.
Roots on the shallow side, occasionally far-reaching –
the story has the lineaments of a classic.

We love intrepid settler stories but lose the plot at real-life struggles.

If camels did play a part in dispersing the plant beyond its native range, they were only one agent in its spread. Trucks, trains, cultivation and climate variables were also factors.

Because it's a (minor) nuisance, there's the mistaken assumption
it's an introduced species,
a snap judgement.
Yet outside
the checks and balances
of its natural habitat
any plant
has the potential
to be weedy.

'The Railway Department had not yet done anything to eradicate the noxious weed, Afghan Thistle, growing on their property ... a most undesirable plant and extremely hard to eradicate when it once gets a hold.'
The Beverley Times, Western Australia, November 1948.
Local radio 1958, a listener phones in with a question.
He wants to know how to get rid of
Afghan thistles.
The expert at the end of the line
refers to Sisyphus.

In the vegetal world thistles – be they true, allied or in name only – are magnificent survivors.

VII

Australia has three native thistles that are out-and-out
thistles, plus a native sow thistle. All belong to the Asteraceae
family.

Sow thistles as a bunch puzzled European explorers and
early scientific travellers to Australia.

'The subject of the southern *Sonchi* allied to the European
S. oleraceus, *asper* and *arvensis*, is involved in much obscurity,
partly owing to these species having been early imported into
all the temperate quarters of the globe and becoming speedily
naturalized; partly to their being truly indigenous in some of
the south-temperate parts of the globe, to which they have
also been imported by man; and most of all to the differences
of opinion that exist as to what are species and what varieties
amongst them, and which are greatly enhanced in the case of
dried specimens.'
The Botany of the Antarctic Voyage, Part 3, *Flora Tasmaniæ*
by Joseph Dalton Hooker, 1860.

In scenes otherwise sepia
there were assertions
followed by counterassertions.
There was equivocation and general uncertainty.

'Probably indigenous to Europe and Temperate Asia,
but now distributed over the greater part of the globe and
perhaps truly indigenous in Australia.'
Flora Australiensis by George Bentham assisted by
Ferdinand von Mueller, 1866.

'In Sydney...it is most commonly known as "cocky weed,"

as it is so frequently gathered for cockatoos…so far as we know, it existed in Australia before the advent of the white man. Hence some botanists look upon it as indigenous, but, bearing in mind its facility of migration (its seeds can be blown across the water for great distances), its colonising power, and the fact that it is not specially Australian in its relationships, it is better, I think, to look upon it as introduced.'

The Weeds of New South Wales by J. H. Maiden, 1920.

They were referring to the common sow thistle because the native species had yet to be identified as such.

*

In 1965 the official botanical name of Australia's native sow thistle was accepted as *Sonchus hydrophilus* Boulos. It has no vernacular name in English but it does in several Aboriginal languages – although whether those words refer specifically to the native species or to sow thistles more broadly is moot.

That's one way to unpack the native–import issue: gather evidence of the plant's presence before European settlement.

Look for sow thistles in Aboriginal vocabularies and dietary practices.

'I remember, as a boy, about 1895,' wrote Adelaide University botanist John Cleland, 'being very much surprised at seeing an insane aboriginal in the Parkside Asylum eat a sow thistle. As I have never seen white people eat these, he could hardly have learnt to eat this plant from whites, and his doing so may have been a relic of his earlier days.'

Look for sow thistles in the accounts of ethnographers and expeditioners who journeyed in remote and isolated regions.

'On the isle is fresh water; and cabbage palm, wood-sorrel, sow thistle, and samphire abounding in some places on the shore, we brought on board as much of each sort as the time we had to gather them would admit.'

A Voyage towards the South Pole, &c. by James Cook, 1777.

But what type of sow thistle was it that Cook observed on Norfolk Island?

Our continent was never quite as isolated as we think it was. Way before Magellan's fleet sailed blind across unknown waters in 1521, Polynesian mariners had struck out into the cauldron of the Pacific on their own voyages of exploration. And going back further, biologists speculate that the seeds of the native *Sonchus* may have been carried by birds migrating from Asia thousands of years ago.

Going back is difficult.

Unless you have herbarium specimens of intact provenance, it's well nigh impossible to determine if early references to sow thistles were to the native species. Or to other members of the *Sonchus* diaspora.

Look-alikes, analogues, peas in a pod, so to speak.

Preserved in correspondence,

in field notes and dried examples

of nineteenth-century logic.

*

The leaves of *Sonchus hydrophilus* are less divided than those of the introduced species and, as its name suggests, the plant favours watery environments: spongy soils, stream banks, lakesides and swamps.

The flowers are yellow, bright

and obvious as a country song.

Somewhere above the clouds

the sound of an aircraft…

From scientific papers I learn about pollen deposits

and phylogenesis – the evolutionary development and diversification of a species. From early botanical texts – the kind where an f might be an s – I pick up evocative turns of phrase and watercolour portraits. I'm not a scientist and truth is there are only so many graphs and algorithms I can plough through before I feel the urge to click the close button on my computer. And rewind...

Here's a description of *Sonchus oleraceus* from the gloriously titled *English Botany or, Coloured Figures of British Plants, with their Essential Characters, Synonyms, and Places of Growth. To which Will be Added, Occasional Remarks*. A set of thirty-six volumes by James Edward Smith and botanical illustrator James Sowerby, issued between 1790 and 1813.

'One of the most common of all weeds in every kind of cultivated land; and like such vagrant annuals it assumes a variety of forms according to the variations of soil and moisture. The flowers are to be met with from midsummer to the end of autumn.'

I read that and all of a sudden I long for imaginary, expatriate England. I fall back into a jigsaw-puzzle picture of bluebells and beech trees and blackberries ripe for the picking. It's a silly, bogus, biologically impossible image (bluebells flower in spring; blackberries fruit late summer and early autumn) but it makes my eyeballs prickle.

Somewhere above the clouds
the sound of an aircraft...

VIII

Spineless. Benign. You may not recognise our native thistles as such because they're not sharp or prickle-covered. I've read somewhere that when the first thistles arrived in Australia they probably did have thorns or spines, but over the millennia they lost them. They weren't needed because there were very few grazing animals. And if you're a plant, that's the point of spikiness – it's a defence mechanism to stop you being eaten.

The austral cornflower, sometimes called simply 'native thistle', churned through a few Latin names and authors before landing at *Rhaponticum australe*.

An understory species, it was once widespread across the grasslands and open eucalypt forests of eastern Australia. It is now extinct in Victoria and New South Wales – a consequence of land clearing for cultivation, livestock and urban development.

It hangs on in southeast Queensland where it maintains small (and vulnerable) populations outside pastoral blankets. On nature strips, rail reserves and patches of remnant ecosystem.

Other threats to *Rhaponticum australe* are habitat fragmentation, weeds, feral horses and – in a kind of evolutionary irony – being eaten by grazing animals. Stock find austral cornflowers, thistles minus spines, immensely palatable.

They tempt not only hungry cattle.

The closely related thistle *Rhaponticum uniflorum*, which is native to Korea and other parts of east Asia, has a history of use in traditional medicine and cookery. Young buds are used in salads while root material is typically cooked.

Before it became scarce, was *R. australe* a food source for Aboriginal people?

*

Austral cornflowers are quite often mistaken for introduced thistles and removed. I've seen them only in photographs and, yes, there is a family resemblance. I find all thistles beautiful. A minority view – at least outside Scotland. But I think many people would find *R. australe* an attractive plant. Could it have a future as an ornamental? Good for gardeners, good for conservation.

Flowering happens late spring and summer; single reddish-pink blooms atop long stems. Once spent, these flowers turn into fluffy, light brown seedheads whose shape and appearance send me straight to Shakespeare. To this much-quoted couplet from *Cymbeline*:

'Golden boys and girls all must

As chimney-sweepers come to dust.'

Shakespeare and his audiences knew their wildflowers. Chimney-sweepers was a local nickname for the seed clocks of dandelions. Austral cornflowers' seedheads are semi-spheres rather than clocks, but brush-like they definitely are. Imagine a —— what's the collective noun for chimney sweepers? A stack? A soot? Imagine a smoulder of miniature chimney sweepers.

Thistledown drifts
from verges and in-between zones
the sites of passage
geographers call liminal.
Seeds airborne in swirls
spindrifts like cappuccino foam,
like a sofa unstuffing ——

Let's stay with sofas for a moment – and how much I loathe them on stage. Ratty brown ones, especially. I often stipulate 'absolutely no sofas' in my production notes at the front of a script. With the exception of an armchair circa 2001, I've managed to keep soft furnishings out of my work. If you want to see couches, go to Ikea.

For me, sets designed around sofas signal a certain type of play and a certain type of theatrical production. Conservative, domestic, predictable. It's an oft-repeated cliché that theatre is a mirror held up to society, and it is – but it's also, at its best, much more than that. A space of metaphor and contradiction, audacious, seductive, provocative, carnivalesque. A space in which players and audience together can probe the sinews and viscera of the social body. If reflection were theatre's sole purpose, it could never be any of these things. It would never question establishment shibboleths, never transcend reality.

*

Thistles are a big tribe with representatives (and relatives) across the globe. The Mediterranean basin and parts of the Near East are particularly rich in species, and it was from there that thistles spread to every continent bar Antarctica. This dispersal most likely happened during one of the colder geological epochs.

Rhaponticum species like the austral cornflower fall within the subtribe known as Centaureinae. *R. australe* is one of only two members of that subtribe regarded as indigenous to Australia – and its occurrence isn't easily explained.

This is where it gets complicated and taxonomic.
Among the family trees
soaring choirs of polysyllables.
Ritual duets
like the one that goes

autochthonous or allochthonous?

The first word means originating in the place where it's found rather than descended from colonists or migrants. The other means something imported into an ecosystem from outside.

Rhaponticum uniflorum is also found in Mongolia, China and Japan. Molecular data and studies in biogeography suggest it's the most likely candidate to be a sister species to *R. australe*. This means that they shared a common ancestor way back when, but at some stage in the evolutionary process the austral cornflower split from its 'sister'.

How did it migrate – by what means and what route?

The assumption goes from Asia to Australia. Is it heresy to ask if the migration could have gone the other way?

Were birds involved?

Seeds drop into the earth and germinate.

Separated by ocean and language, united in thistledom.

This sister-splitting business has led some scientists to express doubts about whether the austral cornflower is truly native to Australia.

'Was it the Aborigines that introduced the plant, and were they motivated by its medicinal properties? Had the species, on the other hand, reached Australia without human intervention, but how would this have been achieved?'

That's from a journal article whose twenty-one word title begins 'Phylogeny of Rhaponticum...' Like many scientific papers it's multi-authored, in this instance by Oriane Hidalgo, Núria Garcia-Jacas, Teresa Garnatje and Alfonso Susanna. Published in the *Annals of Botany*, 2006.

I'm thinking about time scales:
what the goldfish remembered,

that a dog's life goes at the speed of seven,
and mayflies fly a single day.

There's a jellyfish that's biologically immortal. It recycles itself, aging backwards from adult to immature polyp, then reversing, over and over again.

Yew trees were often planted in graveyards, their ever-greenness and longevity symbols of resurrection and eternity.

Geological time is – well, geological.

How long do you have to be in a place before you belong? Before you're considered a native.

How many generations does it take to drop the hyphen from your national identity?

For a plant to qualify as indigenous?

IX
Picture the Prussian, the sky blue, the map a fiction where it wasn't blank.

terra firma
mimicking the intrinsics
of the ocean.
Was it here the tide turned?

mare incognitum
aping its prehistory
in mirage and posthumous violet.
Was it here the tide turned –
and he was sunk?

Actites megalocarpus.
The earliest herbarium specimen of this particular native thistle was collected from Queensland's Moreton Bay in 1843 by the explorer and naturalist Ludwig Leichhardt.

You'll find the dune thistle, sometimes called beach thistle or coastal sow thistle, in shoreline environments, on dunes and exposed cliffs around southern and eastern Australia. A perennial species that often grows in the shelter of larger shrubs, it's one tough and resilient plant.
A frontline plant.
It can weather salt-spray,
sand-blasting winds
and full sun.
Flowers are bright yellow, leaves fleshy and stem-hugging. And although they look sharp, they're not.
Actites is a uniquely Australian genus, the dune thistle its

sole species. In appearance and biology it's very similar to plants of the *Sonchus* genus.

A scanty littoral welds sea and sky.

Landward from the shallows, you see a tumble of sand hills, an improvised road and, beyond it, a golf course. You see beach houses hung about with towels, scribbles of seaweed, abandoned shoes. When evening falls, pop ballads drift from open windows and the air gets soupy with exhaust fumes from four-wheel drives racing up and down the beach.

Gulls dodge. Waves crash. A golf ball overshoots the fairway and rolls into a clump of thistles.

The dunes are an unfinished edge, forever in flux.

The dune thistles tell a story older than the beach houses, older than the coastline. Old inhabitants of an old land.

When you see a plant like the dune thistle you probably think weed.

When I hear the name Ludwig Leichhardt, I think inland sea.

Acres of print and gigabytes of web space have been devoted to how Australian nature confounded European explorers and early settlers. Trees shed bark not leaves, swans were black – and rivers flowed inland. In the early 1800s this inside-out geography bolstered the belief that in the heart of the continent lay a vast inland sea, a southern hemisphere Caspian. During the first half of the century the promise of this sea – or a great north-draining river – spurred adventurers and men of science to explore the interior.

The mystery at the centre of Australia defied European logic.

'My dearest brother-in-law.—— Four months have passed since I informed you about my return from Peak Range. I have utilised this time to equip for a new journey, and I will be ready in a few days' time to penetrate again the interior of Australia, and, if God pleases, to cross the whole continent.'

Letter from Leichhardt to his brother-in-law in Germany, February 1848.

Two months later his party set out.

Gone west from Queensland's Darling Downs.

'I have a strange idea that there is a central sea not far from the Banks of the Darling in 29° L. I should go fully prepared for a *voyage*', wrote Charles Sturt in 1844. (Quoted in *The Water Dreamers: The Remarkable History of Our Dry Continent* by Michael Cathcart, 2010.)

Sturt survived to tell his tale. Leichhardt wasn't so lucky.

He and his team disappeared and, despite numerous searches, despite countless theories, nothing was ever found of them. Not a buckle, not a button, not a bone. The German explorer vanished into legend. Only to resurface in poems, novels, plays and a whole literature of misjudged journeys into uncharted territories of earth and soul.

'The imagination has its own geography which alters with the centuries', wrote Graham Greene in a 1952 book review.

In 1957 Leichhardt returned to haunt us as Patrick White's awkward, aloof Johann Ulrich Voss.

'He is going on this great expedition,' says one of the characters. 'You know, to find an inland sea. Or is it gold?'

X

I'm calling this one the ghost thistle – or perhaps the fugitive thistle. It has no common name, so I've decided to give it one.

It was only by accident that I found out about the existence of this particular Australian native.

'There are only two species of Cardueae recorded as native to Australia – *Rhaponticum australe* (Gaudich.) Sojak…and *Hemistepta lyrata* Bunge. The recorded range of *H. lyrata* is from northern NSW to Qld, and Asia. Searches of possible sites in the 1980s, based on herbarium records, failed to find any plants.'

Biological Control of Weeds in Australia 1960 to 2010 edited by Mic Julien, Rachel McFadyen and Jim Cullen, 2012.

I went looking for details and photographs. Here's a précis of what I discovered:

It has a cluster of synonyms. Perhaps most importantly, it was previously classified as *Saussurea*, a genus of some three hundred species native to temperate Eurasia and North America. The earliest Australian specimen was collected by Leichhardt in 1843 and catalogued as *Saussurea carthamoides*.

Or so I thought.

When I read that *H. lyrata* was recorded from the Newcastle area by Robert Brown in 1804, I went looking for it in his diary. Only to find a conundrum. From the plants he collected in that part of New South Wales, I found no *Hemisteptia* (or *Saussurea*) but '*Rhaponticum hermaphroditum*', which the compilers of the diary translate as *Stemmacantha australis*, a synonym for the austral cornflower.

That's one for the scientists to resolve.

Reading Brown's log, my attention strays – from botany to earlier entries itemising his meals and reading matter. It's

July in the North Atlantic, the gusts are gale force and he's got a sore throat, but neither storm nor sickness affect his appetite. He tucks into corned beef, mutton, salt cod, cabbage and potatoes, drinks generous quantities of wine and port, and rounds off his evenings with Shakespeare.

'Historically recorded from numerous places in northern coastal NSW...Since 1955, collected only from central southern Qld. It inhabits creekbanks or low-lying areas on alluvial flats.'

Flora of Australia, volume 37, 2015.

'A cursory examination of the distribution of *H. lyrata*...would suggest that it is quite a common and/or widespread species', wrote A. R. Bean in a 1999 article, 'Notes on Hemisteptia lyrata (Asteraceae) and its Australian occurrence'. But scratch the surface and the lack of recent examples probably 'reflects a drastic decline in the total population and distribution of the species in Australia'.

It grows to a maximum height of around a metre and its flowers are a purply shade of pink. Bean describes it as 'an erect unarmed daisy'.

It may be a new thistle to me, and not much noticed in Australia, but *H. lyrata* is prevalent in a lot of places. From India to Manchuria, Southeast Asia to Japan. In Taiwan it grows on waste ground, roadsides, rice-paddy ridges and cultivated lower-lands up to altitudes of eight hundred metres. According to Korean researchers, it has a history not only as a medicinal herb, but also – in one of those off-centre translations I love – as a 'mountainous vegetable'.

There are articles about its chemistry and pharmacological properties from scientists in China and South Korea, but mostly what I discovered is that information about this species is sparse.

Contradictory, too.

A Queensland Government website lists the plant as native and its conservation status as 'Least Concern'.

Flora of Australia has it as endangered.

Like the austral cornflower, because there's a sizeable gap or disjunction in its distribution, there's a grain or two of doubt about its native status.

In 2005 Biosecurity Australia had it down as an 'Exotic Plant Species' given the green light for import into the country.

*

Somewhere along the line, I spotted that extra i. I'd been searching for *Hemistepta lyrata*, when the accepted botanical name is *Hemisteptia lyrata* (plus authorial credits). This wasn't a typo or spelling mistake on my part; the plant appears as *Hemistepta*-no-i in many references, current as well as historical.

Perhaps its common name should be iThistle?

Whatever name I make up for it, in Australia *H. lyrata* is a spectral presence. With or without the second i.

I for insubstantial.

I for invisible.

What does it mean to be invisible? Is it a condition between rare and extinct? Is it the same thing as transparency?

Architects have designed a so-called invisible skyscraper for construction near South Korea's Incheon Airport. The idea is to project onto its surface what you would see if the tower weren't there.

'Yesterday, upon the stair,

I met a man who wasn't there...'

Invisibility is the stuff of riddles and fairytales, of religions, of science fiction – and science fact. We've invented microscopes, X-rays, telescopes and other technologies to reveal otherwise hidden features of our bodies and our cosmos. Our world is one of computers and smartphones, of electronic devices activated by signals and fields that are invisible to us.

In drama and fiction power corrupts, but invisibility can be every bit as corrosive. Elizabethan and early Jacobean theatre are full of apparitions and spooky manifestations.

Macbeth clutches at an invisible dagger, all the while wondering – in one of the play's most famous soliloquies – whether it's real or 'a false creation', the product of his 'heat-oppressed brain'. In the following act the ghost of the murdered Banquo appears during a royal feast. Invisible to Lady Macbeth and the assembled company, Banquo's 'horrible shadow' so agitates Macbeth the dinner guests are sent home early.

Camouflage is a tilt at invisibility, often aping nature's tricks. *Macbeth* again. In the final act Malcolm's soldiers disguise themselves with tree branches and so does 'Birnam wood remove to Dunsinane'. In contemporary productions Birnham wood is more likely to come to Dunsinane by means of digital projection.

Get past the magic cloaks and stealth jets and being invisible may simply mean being overlooked or ignored.

Take political protests – and I've been on a few.

The issues are perennial.

A bunch of us stand for hours in the sun

like small carnations
sanguine in the heat-sick air
getting pinker by the minute.
The world's furious songs in our veins
we listen to a string of monologues
while security guards stare through mirrored shades
and surveillance cameras snap us for the record.

Thinking about invisibility might tell us something about the composition of society. About the material and the intangible. It might encourage us to speak out when the Emperor's new clothes are obviously a scam and he's parading around in his underpants.

Here's a totally arbitrary shortlist of invisible things:
Gravity.
Morality.
Stick insects.
The Cheshire Cat.
Mathematical concepts.
Middle-aged women.
Abstract thought.
Wallflowers and ghost thistles.

'The true mystery of the world is the visible, not the invisible.'
The Picture of Dorian Gray by Oscar Wilde, 1891.

FOOD

HOW TO EAT A THISTLE

I was thirteen when I ate my first thistle.

I didn't recognise it as such. In fact, I didn't recognise it, period.

It was handed to me on a plate, along with a dish of vinaigrette, during a school exchange visit to France. I had no idea what it was, and absolutely no idea how to eat this thing that looked – well, like a hand grenade.

My host family was already tucking in, removing leaves one by one and dipping them in the sauce. I did the same, pulled off a leaf, doused it, put it in my mouth and chewed.

And chewed and chewed.

To say it was stringy would be an understatement. Imagine eating a doormat. I was composing a polite French excuse when I noticed piles of discarded leaves on everyone else's plates. And realised they were eating only the creamy base, not the whole leaf thing that I was trying so hard to swallow.

I copied them. And discovered the artichoke.

It may be the most frequently eaten thistle, but the globe artichoke, *Cynara scolymus* in Latin, doesn't exist in the wild. It's a domesticated expression of the cardoon, or possibly another member of the *Cynara* genus. There are differing accounts of its origin.

Some cite north Africa as its birthplace.

Others suggest Sicily.

Historians and food writers agree, however, that by the fifteenth century the vegetable in its modern form had arrived in Italy. From where it spread north and west to France.

Avignon, 1532. Artichokes appeared on the public record.

They figured in an ode by Pierre de Ronsard, circa 1554.

Voltaire cultivated them in his kitchen garden.

And in the village of Saint-Georges du Bois, I encountered them for the first time.

This was the beginning of a long love affair

with all things French.

The headmaster of my high school was an advocate of interactive language teaching before interactive became the buzzword it is today. In practice this meant we learnt French not by the textbook, but by listening and speaking. And we learnt fast enough that, a couple of years in, I could stop reading novels in translation and start reading them in their original language – well, the short, modern ones. The nineteenth century would have to wait.

The school's approach was also, to use another buzzword, immersive. There were productions of plays by Molière and Camus, films from the French New Wave (where we discovered there was more to l'amour than adolescent fumbling), and every year some of us participated in an exchange with a school in the town of Surgères. It worked like this:

You were paired with a student of the same age, gender and height.

For three weeks you lived with their family, and for three they stayed with yours.

Fast-forward to the present and I'm foraging in the seams of Pyrmont. A fat tongue of land that was once Sydney's maritime heartland. I'm after sow thistles, specifically *Sonchus oleraceus*.

On the Anzac Bridge above, tiny fluorescent men maintain something or other. The air has a metallic tang. Remember when you were little and put a toy car in your mouth? It tastes like that. I don't think I'll be eating any sow thistles growing here.

*

I assumed that artichokes came to Australia with migrants from southern Europe. Were part of the horticultural and culinary diversification associated with postwar immigration.

But that turned out to be a fallacy.

The globe artichoke was the first documented exotic thistle to arrive in Australia. It arrived with the First Fleet and by July 1788 was growing on Norfolk Island. 'Every vegetable at the plantation was in a thriving state,' reported Lieutenant King, 'turneps, carrots, lettuces of three sorts, onions, leeks, parsley, cellery, five sorts of cabbages, corn sallad, artichokes, and beet in great forwardness'.

By December 1827 the globe artichoke and the cardoon were both on the 'List of esculent vegetables and pott herbs cultivated in the Botanic Gardens, Sydney'.

Two years later artichokes were selling for 3d apiece at the Sydney Markets.

They received regular mention in farmers' calendars, gardening columns and horticultural literature.

They were on the menu of a Sydney hotel in 1855.

The handbook *How to Settle in Victoria* included them in its inventory of culinary plants 'best adapted to the Australian climate' and Ferdinand von Mueller recommended their extended cultivation.

Yet we have this tendency to imagine the past as less vibrant than the present, leached of colour, intensity and, yes, even vegetables.

The name 'thistle' encompasses a large group of plants

classified and divided by botanists along various lines. Here's one arrangement:

Artichokes and cardoons are in the spiny thistle category, along with the fierce, purple-flowered plants we typically associate with the word thistle.

Chicory or soft thistles tell a different story. Yellow flowers, milky sap and spineless. Usually.

Sow thistles fall on the soft side.

They come in different varieties, but all are part of the genus *Sonchus*. The one most often devoured by humans is *Sonchus oleraceus*, the common sow thistle.

For the artichoke's wild progenitor, *Cynara cardunculus*, it was probably a combination of accident and design that brought it to Australia. The earliest record of the cardoon or artichoke thistle I can find is from July 1836, in the catalogue of a Hobart nursery.

By 1879 it was naturalised in South Australia.

It came somewhat later to Victoria but spread rapidly. Stands of cardoons first established themselves on the outskirts of Melbourne. From where enterprising residents harvested their blooms to sell in the city's Queen Victoria Market as 'Scotch thistles'. The sale of these plants was illegal. At Preston local court in 1929, Mr H. W. Henkel, an Inspector with the Vermin and Noxious Weeds Department, produced a seven-and-a-half foot specimen as evidence of wrongdoing.

*

Surgères was, probably still is, a quiet provincial town. Inland from the Atlantic port of La Rochelle, unhurried amid the agricultural flatness of Charente-Maritime. My exchange partner, Jacqueline B——, lived five kilometres out of

Surgères in Saint-Georges du Bois, population approximately 1,500. Her father had a small holding, Madame B—— ran the village grocery, while a black-clad devil of a grandmother barked orders in a kind of dialect, but cooked like an angel.

To prepare an artichoke requires patience. Jane Grigson saw them as a counterpoint to the dash and fast-food ethos of contemporary life. While I appreciate Grigson's sentiment, her recipes are elaborate, and the two-and-a-half pages on methods of tackling artichokes somewhat off-putting. I've noticed this discouraging tendency in other cookbooks; artichokes require commitment and a high degree of culinary confidence. Subtext: the novice or casual cook should hone their skills on more pedestrian vegetables before graduating to artichokes.

'It is good for a man to eat thistles, and to remember that he is an ass. But an artichoke is the best of thistles.' Those two sentences begin E. S. Dallas's much cited entry in *Kettner's Book of the Table*. What follows is less often repeated: 'There are several elaborate ways of dressing the artichoke…Each is a mountain of labour for a mouse of result.' The artichoke acquired a reputation as difficult. A fiddly, time-consuming vegetable best left in the too-hard basket.

In most of the mass market cookery books produced in the early and mid-twentieth century, the alphabet begins with A for asparagus, not artichoke.

The Davey Flour Mill is a shell of itself. Enclosed, awaiting its rebirth as an apartment complex. Bound by the Western Distributor and Sydney's light rail line, it's packed for now with verdant weeds.

I squeeze through a gap in the fencing.

The plants are covered with some kind of dust from the

building. I'm wondering if it contains lead from old paint. Also wondering about pesticides. And of course, dog piss.

I'm not even entirely sure why I'm here. Is it the city dweller's desire to connect with nature and its seasonal rhythms? The appeal of lunch picked from wasteland instead of the supermarket shelf? Maybe it's a childhood memory:

Go on, I dare you--

Hide and seek from grown-ups, scanning the field, challenging each other to eat a leaf or berry.

Or maybe it's my peasant DNA kicking in? The same DNA that used to make my mother stop the car in the middle of nowhere and shin up a tree to collect fungi. In her sensible Marks & Spencer handbag she always carried a penknife, secateurs and a wad of plastic and paper bags.

I think about relationships
between domestic species and their distant relatives.

Skip-read potted histories of commercial artichoke farming in California. Itinerant workers with bent backs and calloused hands and prospects as threadbare as their jeans. Characters ripped from the pages of a John Steinbeck novel.

The artichoke may have gone in and out of fashion and favour, not so the cardoon. After a brief moment in the sun it was demoted from vegetable to weed.

1847: *The South Australian Register* described it as 'the garden artichoke in degeneracy'.

Language offers both connection and rupture. One person's weed is another's meal. The cardoon, wrote W. T. Parsons, 'is so closely related to Globe Artichoke that many New Australians collect heads from the heavy infestations around Melbourne and treat them in the same way as Globe Artichoke'.

The Journal of Agriculture, Victoria, September 1959.

Another name for the cardoon is artichoke thistle. And to the layperson the globe artichoke and cardoon are hard to distinguish. A difference of semitones.

Artichoke thistle.

That name sets it squarely in the weeds camp.

As a thistle the plant is an unpalatable alien, good for nothing, a barrier to human enterprise and expansion.

As a cardoon…

Food, but not as we know it. Even its name sounds odd and vaguely comic, a cross between cartoon and buffoon. Picture an animated version running amok across the screen, a slapstick vegetable if ever there was one.

In Spain, Italy and southern France, cardoons are prepared in a variety of ways. Although the buds can be eaten, dishes from the anchovy belt of the Mediterranean rely on the leaf stalks. These might be tossed in olive oil or butter, baked au gratin or served in a broth with meatballs.

Marcel Proust's narrator remembered not only those famous madeleines, but also cardoons with marrow, prepared by the family cook as a Sunday treat.

But, as Grigson points out, the cardoon never caught on in Britain. An indifference shared by the English-speaking world.

Although Australians shunned cardoons for human consumption, the plant had its advocates, who argued it made decent animal fodder. Debate was heated and some extravagant assertions were made. A parliamentarian and sometime correspondent for the *Advertiser* claimed, in 1910, to have seen cows climb trees in order to eat the flowerheads.

*

Happenstance plants, fortuitous flora, weeds, wild greens – however you label them, sow thistles are unequivocal and hugely successful anthropophytes; i.e., plants that travel with humans, moving in wherever we till or otherwise disturb the earth.

Their origin is variously given as Europe, the Mediterranean basin, areas of Africa and Asia. And they're now almost ubiquitous. Sow thistles are happy downtown or bush, inland, lowland, along the coast or up a hill.

They've thrust their prickled snouts

into Greenland's icy southern edge.

And even desert habitats.

Perennial, rough, clammy and common. The informal nomenclature may be disputed; their early arrival is not.

Sonchus oleraceus was recorded by Robert Brown, the botanist who circumnavigated with Flinders.

In 1843 James Drummond, one-time Western Australian Government Naturalist, wrote: 'The English sow thistle, which was quite unknown here when the colony was first established is now spread over the whole face of the country.'

Many early travellers commented on their size and luxuriance: 'The Sow thistles were 15 feet high in many places.'

(At a mere half-metre, my Pyrmont specimens are positively anorexic.)

Settlers found them 'very little inferior to cauliflowers or cabbage.'

Like boiled spinach, said some.

A prohibited pest more like, said others.

Speaking for myself, there's something delicious about eating a plant with an outlaw history.

*

Like other vegetables lost from the modern portfolio, the cardoon connects to long traditions of nurturing and breeding. And to the migration of people and culture.

In the 1990s I interviewed women from non-English speaking backgrounds as part of a playwriting commission. This anecdote didn't make the final draft but I remember it well. An interviewee told me one of her memories of growing up in Adelaide was cringing in the back seat of the family car while her Italian-born parents snuck into strangers' yards, and even their Aussie neighbours' yards, at night to collect cardoons that would otherwise go to waste.

Artichokes returned to Australian tables after the end of World War II with the influx of migrants hungry for familiar foods and with the know-how to produce them on a profitable scale. Helped by a more epicurean approach to dining and a desire to explore foreign foodways.

In *Continental Cookery in Australia*, one of the first locally published books on the subject, Maria Koszlik Donovan informed her readers that 'nowhere do cooks do greater justice to this luscious variety of the thistle than in Italy'.

Although books, newspapers and magazines printed recipes for goulash and minestrone and Linzer torte, Australia's continental drift had a strong French flavour. To the Anglosphere, French lent not only food-related language but also a soupçon of chic, and if you were unsure how to eat an artichoke, this 1952 book *Oh, for a French Wife!* supplied instruction:

'Take those tender inner leaves and dip them into the hot melted butter which we have spooned onto each plate; then each leaf slides between our closed teeth, leaving behind its delicately flavoured pulp.'

Oh, if only I'd read that before my trip to France.

My first contact with cardoons was at a midweek market in Surgères. The stalls were spread with lush bouquets of herbs quite unlike the measly sprigs in plastic coffins you buy in supermarkets. Scents of thyme and earth packed the air. Jacqueline and I trailed along behind her grandmother and some old crony, trying to put as much distance between us and them as possible. Until Grandmère B—— summoned us to carry her purchases. She handed me an armful of what looked like killer celery.

I asked her what it was.

'Les cardons,' she replied.

I was none the wiser.

Back in Saint-Georges du Bois, Jacqueline's mother explained that dried cardoon flowers were added to warm milk to make it curdle. Grandmère B—— used them to make the soft cheese that was a speciality of the Charentes.

If this all sounds like some kind of rustic or gastronomic idyll, it wasn't – not for a teenage girl with bohemian aspirations. Reality went like this: no bathroom; once a week you went to the public bathhouse for a shower. Entertainment comprised non-stop TV every evening and Sundays visiting sick and dead relatives in hospitals and cemeteries. And no one in the family had ever in their entire lives been to Paris.

This was not the France of de Beauvoir and Sartre and May '68.

Below the window of the first-floor bedroom I shared with Jacqueline, a flat roof and adjoining wall offered a convenient (and clandestine) nocturnal exit.

The official activities laid on for us included a trip to a Cognac distillery – can you imagine a school doing that now? – and a son et lumière show about Hélène de Surgères, one of Catherine de Médici's ladies-in-waiting and Pierre de Ronsard's sometime muse.

Unofficially, I was hitchhiking into town. Hoping like crazy no one saw me getting into strangers' cars and told the school or my host family what I was doing.

First one café, then another. And another. A bunch of us sampling the bottles behind the bar, spending the little bit of money we had as fast as we could. Until were were ——

Sick. Sick. Sick as dogs.

After that particular débâcle there was an emergency confab of teachers and parents. They imposed a curfew.

They were kidding themselves.

We were fifteen, sixteen stupid years old.

*

Part of the vernacular landscape, sow thistles are also a part of culinary lexicons. From Africa to Greece to China – and across the Pacific.

When the English botanist Joseph Hooker visited New Zealand in 1841, he reported that sow thistles were eaten by the local Maori.

One of humankind's survival foods, they sustained Indigenous Australians and hungry explorers alike.

The leaves are rich in minerals and vitamin C.

'Yesterday we obtained a few sow-thistles, which we boiled, and found to be very good', wrote John McDouall Stuart in 1858.

Almost thirteen years earlier Charles Sturt, seriously ill with scurvy, prayed for rain 'to make the herbage spring, as sow thistles and other plants would be an excellent substitute for common culinary herbs'.

John Lhotsky, the Lviv-born naturalist and radical, observed the tribes of the Monaro in southeast New

South Wales eating 'a root of a sort of Sonchus'. While South Australian settler Edward Stephens recalled how an Aboriginal party asked permission to harvest a large plot of sow thistles on the land he occupied. Take the lot, he told them. And 'ten minutes later the ground was bare of thistles, and the tribe passed on gratefully devouring the juicy weed'.

On a less tangible note...

The departed souls of the Kurnai people from Gippsland were said to live on sow thistles.

*

We've moved from bottoms to hearts.

Cookery books of the eighteenth and nineteenth centuries nearly always refer to artichoke bottoms, as does this 1767 recipe for a ragout which starts with the direction 'take twelve bottoms, soften them in warm water...'

By the 1960s, however, when tins and jars of preserved artichokes began to appear on the shelves of delicatessens and the more adventurous grocers, they were unequivocally hearts.

Take even a perfunctory glance at those old cookbooks and you soon realise that once upon a time we ate a lot of thistles. Alongside multiple varieties of artichoke and cardoon, the encyclopaedic 1919 *Sturtevant's Edible Plants of the World* lists a further seven esculent thistles. And they give generously of themselves.

Leaves, shoots and stems.

Roots.

Buds and flower receptacles.

Back to the cosmopolitan sow thistle.

Mentioned indirectly in the Old Testament, it is one of the five bitter herbs named by the Mishnah (a collection of interpretations of Jewish law that constitutes part of the Talmud) to be eaten on the night of the Passover Seder, that extended ritual of memory and feasting. To recall the bitterness of the Israelites' servitude in Egypt.

According to sociologist Arthur W. Frank, when we tell personal stories we often 'hitch a ride' on pre-existing tales. He cites an example of someone borrowing the Exodus narrative to describe a voyage from Europe to New York on which the majority of passengers were refugees.

Plants also piggy-back.

Theseus apparently scoffed a dish of sow thistles before tackling the Minotaur.

Or is it the other way around? Do plants sprout their own myths and folklore? The dark sayings of nature, as Ruskin called them.

*

I've got my eye on number 21 Harris Street, Pyrmont.

I suspect sow thistles may be growing behind the fence. The site was a wartime engineering workshop but it's vacant land now, the building long demolished. Getting inside will be tricky though. Unlike my mother, I don't carry bolt cutters in my backpack.

During the war Mum picked sow thistles to supplement rations. As have people down the centuries.

We live in an age of mass transplantation. Sow thistles, cardoons and hundreds of other species are now comfortably at home in the New World.

When we move, be it ten kilometres down the road or across the globe, we take with us our culinary and environmental attachments, favourite recipes and wayside knowledge.

To remind us of home, yes, but also to help us adapt to the

new places in which we find ourselves.

Lantana, grasses, small dust-flowers, peepholes, wire, sow thistles flagrant with seed. Which means they're past it. You need young leaves. After washing them – in water with a splash of vinegar to remove any nasties – I blanche them to reduce their natural bitterness. Some people eat sow thistles raw in salads but I prefer them cooked. In a frittata where their sharpness lifts the rounded flavours of eggs and potatoes. In a colcannon. Or with tofu and spring onions in a *jjigae*, a soupy Korean stew that I eat with a bowl of rice and kimchi.

Post school I continued travelling to France. Weekends in Paris; camping holidays in Brittany; grape-picking in the Loire Valley; a field trip to the Basque country where I tried to turn my research sweepings into a coherent thesis. After that my enthusiasm for France and everything French waned. My focus shifted. I was accepted into a Masters program in South American studies and, although I eventually declined that offer to take up a postgraduate scholarship at London University, my interest in more distant lands endured.

We all have one, according to Pierre Bayard, psychoanalyst and professor of French literature. An 'inner library' that is the sum of the books we read, talk about and forget.

Those adolescent exchanges to France taught me new vocabularies of swear words and vegetables.

Such that my journey to – let's be generous and call it sophistication – involved not only dreaming of Simone and Jean-Paul and passionate debate in Left Bank cafés (although I did my share of that), but also the eating of grown-up vegetables. The thistle was implicated in culture and in the life I wanted for myself as an adult. It still is.

FORGOTTEN ROOTS

I

In Portugal and Spain it's leaves. In France it all comes down to roots.

The land rises and falls in modest measure. Wheat fields and wide horizons. Pocket orchards of citrus and stone fruit, cork oaks, straggles of thyme. One of Europe's least populated parts, the province of Alentejo in southern Portugal has large expanses of uncultivated or semi-cultivated terrain where golden thistles spurt yellow over the scrub. Although the practice has waned in recent decades, these wild thistles are still gathered and their leaves, midribs and stems used in cooking.

The story is similar in neighbouring Spain.

'In Spain, the golden thistle is used differently from France, where only the roots are eaten', wrote the authors of *Le potager d'un curieux* (*A Curious Person's Kitchen Garden*), a late nineteenth-century compendium of edible plants from France, its colonies and elsewhere. A trove of information about rare, unusual and little-known species. The authors, Auguste Pailleux and Désiré Bois, wax rhapsodic about the golden thistle. There isn't an English edition of *Le potager d'un curieux*, so this is my rough translation:

'If there is a vegetable that deserves to be carefully cultivated, but on the contrary, is neglected and almost abandoned in some areas, it is certainly the golden thistle. It seems to me that no other vegetable, ancient or new, possesses as many qualities...I consider it able to compete without too great a disadvantage not only with the closely related scorzonera or salsify, but with cardoons and cauliflower, those vegetables to which gardeners devote all their attention.'

Many thistles have edible roots, but those most commonly eaten come from the golden thistle (*Scolymus hispanicus*). Often called Spanish oyster plant or Spanish salsify because its flavour is apparently akin to that of salsify. The parsnip-like taproot of the spotted golden thistle (*Scolymus maculatus*) is similarly palatable, although on the Iberian peninsula where it grows wild it is – like its golden relative – harvested primarily for its leaves.

That's not to say that everyone finds them toothsome. In *Don Quixote,* when the Squire of the Woods explains to Sancho that, 'my stomach isn't made for thistles or wild pears or forest roots', we know that Cervantes means golden or spotted golden thistles. Because the Spanish word he uses is not the generic *cardos* but the Scolymus-specific *tagarninas*.

*

'Another bad weed for New South Wales.'

In a 1908 article J. H. Maiden wrote that *Scolymus maculatus*, the spotted golden thistle, 'was evidently cultivated only for its beauty, but not for any economic value. Indeed, I cannot find any redeeming feature except its picturesqueness.' A judgement echoed by the manager of Warrah Station in the northeastern part of the state, who told Maiden that he had been aware of the thistles' existence on his property for at least fourteen years. 'We, of course, destroy it', he said, 'otherwise I feel sure it would soon take possession. Nothing will either eat it or approach it; it is, in fact, the most worthless and most dangerous plant I have ever met with belonging to the thistle family'.

'Importers of plants would do well to be careful as to what members of the Composite family they introduce here. Many of these vegetable pests were no doubt brought out in the first instance by enthusiasts, with a view to perpetuate the memories of their homes in the old country. We noticed the other day the Scolymus, the variety of thistle known in Europe as the golden thistle, planted in a garden as an ornament. It requires no great pretensions to prophecy to enable any one to predict that at no distant date its descendants will be all over the colony.'

The Sydney Mail and New South Wales Advertiser, March 1871.

A Mediterranean native, there are stretches of golden thistle in California, Chile and Argentina, but only in Australia is it considered a troublesome weed and even here its distribution is limited to parts of Victoria. (The spotted version is found only in northern New South Wales.)

The golden thistle was first documented as a garden escapee from the Melbourne suburb of Toorak in 1901, but precisely how and when it arrived in this country is unclear.

It was listed in American seed catalogues of the 1880s and, according to W. T. Parsons, 'was probably imported as a garden vegetable, although it could have been introduced accidentally in hay or chaff'.

The Journal of Agriculture, Victoria, September 1958.

Nor is it known how it got to central Victoria, although Parsons notes that most of the areas where it occurs were once gold-mining districts.

That may be relevant. Or not.

*

Inland Alentejo is hot and dry. On its undulating plains

cattle kick up circuses of dust and olive trees stand their ground. In sun-smacked villages life follows the rhythm of regional songs. The two-part singing of Cante Alentejano is traditionally performed by amateur choirs of agricultural workers or miners. The lyrics speak of love, labour, local saints and the character of this semi-arid corner of the world. But in the music you can hear the influence of the Moors who ruled southern Portugal for over five hundred years. That Arab influence is also present in the food and cooking of Alentejo. In its use of herbs and spices, and in dishes made with foraged produce.

The culinary (and medicinal) virtues of wild thistles were known across north Africa; the plants featured in salads, snacks and tagines. The thirteenth-century compilation *Hispano-Maghreb Cooking during the Almohad Period* includes recipes for sweet thistle paste and a syrup of thistles.

Portuguese thistle recipes include bean or chickpea dishes, bread soups with cod, and cozido, a rustic stew combining a selection of meats (beef, offal, fatty salt pork, smoked sausage) with potatoes, carrots, cabbage and, when available, golden thistles.

The rural calendar persists.

Ethnobotanical studies describe the collecting of golden thistles for home consumption and for sharing with neighbours and family. The plants are also bundled up and sold in local markets, and to urban chefs keen to experiment with funky ingredients.

Folk tales and proverbs supply historical context.

Patterns of wild-plant use change because of associations with poverty and times of hardship. (During the Spanish Civil War golden thistles were a valued food resource.) Because agricultural practices change. Because people move or migrate. Because kids get driven to school instead of walking, thereby missing out on contact with nature. Because traditional knowledge is lost.

II

Contemporary cookbooks come with stories. But sometimes I want only the recipe.

No reminiscing, no personal narrative, no slice of grandma's whatever.

Sometimes I want those jazz-like recipes you find in older cookbooks that assume you've grasped the basics and know how to improvise.

No quantities, no timings, no step by careful step.

Just— —

'Carefully wash and remove shoots from the salsify. Place it in boiling stock and boil till tender. Serve very hot in a vegetable dish either with a white sauce or with a little melted butter over it in two lots as they must not be crowded.'

That's from *A Handbook of Cookery for a Small House* by Jessie Conrad, wife of Polish-born, French-speaking, English-writing novelist Joseph. Published in 1923, with a preface by Joseph, we learn that Jessie spends a mere five hours a day in the kitchen preparing meals, with the assistance of a single maid! I find the recipes unappealing – way too much smothering in thick, floury sauce – but her husband's circle considered her an excellent cook.

Cooking aside, the literati found the Conrads' relationship unfathomable and Jessie was frequently criticised for her weight, her phlegmatic disposition and her working-class origins. H. G. Wells called her 'a Flemish thing from the mud flats', and in a diary entry Virginia Woolf famously referred to her as Conrad's 'lump of a wife'.

Yet Joseph's letters give a rather different portrait of a marriage. In 1916 he wrote from Glasgow: 'You are in every way a dear and very fine creature my own Jess'. Signed off, 'Ever Your devoted lover'. At that point they'd been together twenty years.

In 1920 the Conrads' financial dreams were riding on Joseph's silent 'film-play' *Gaspar the Strong Man*. A cinematic adaptation of his short story *Gaspar Ruiz*.

In 1923 they hoped *A Handbook of Cookery for a Small House* would prove lucrative.

'There have been some very good notices in the *Tatler* and one or two other papers of the little book. There was also an offer to me from a big London Magazine to take over the whole cookery side.' Jessie to Joseph, April 1923.

The screenplay was never produced.

Another fact: Mrs Heart of Darkness penned not one but two cookbooks. The second, *Home Cookery*, was published in January 1936. I read it in the British Library the last time I was in London. Several recipes in this collection have a foreign flavour: German soup, Shrimps à la Mexico, Corsican potatoes, Russian cream, Viennese pudding, Polish sour cream cake, Swedish buns, etc.

In the foreword, Jessie explains that, 'these notes were made and collected during many years. It was my much esteemed privilege to be allowed to penetrate into the kitchen on the few occasions when my husband and I have managed to get a short holiday abroad'.

III

Golden thistles pop up regularly in French botanicals of the nineteenth century. Horticultural trials were producing larger, fleshier roots, but the core problem remained.

'The presence of a "cord" that was probably an obstacle to the success of this vegetable, because its root shares with that of skirret the possession of a fibrous, inedible centre that must be removed before or after cooking.'

Histoire des légumes by Georges Gibault, 1912.

Nevertheless— —

Gardeners and gastronomes sang in unison: *Vive le scolyme dans le potager!*

'In France, we should cultivate the golden thistle more', urged Gibault. 'This culinary root deserves to become something other than a vegetable oddity.'

Botany may distinguish true roots from rhizomes and tubers but we group them all together as root vegetables. True roots include carrots, beetroot, radishes, golden thistles and the wonderfully medieval-sounding mangle-wurzel.

Root vegetables are peasant food
or animal fodder;
lugubrious songs
pulled from the earth;
weather-coloured sputniks
that taste of winter.

My mother came of age during World War II, and its privations shaped her life. She darned socks and recycled threadbare sheets by cutting them in half and sewing them sides to middle. She rinsed polythene bags for re-use and hoarded rubber bands – because you never know when you might need them.

In 1942 the UK Ministry of Food issued the Emergency

Powers Defence (Food) Carrots Order and tried to persuade the public that carrots were a delicious, nutritious, easy-to-grow substitute for rationed goods. Radio programs, competitions, leaflets and cartoon characters were deployed to sell the message.

Carrot scramble, anyone?

My first ever theatrical appearance was as a carrot. In what I always assumed was a harvest pageant. But Mum said, no, it was the school nativity play. I'm not sure where vegetables figure in the birth of Jesus but there we were, a chorus of legumes and taproots in that Bethlehem stable. We rehearsed in a chilly, rattle-bag classroom. I wanted to be the angel Gabriel but was given the choice of parsnip or carrot, and went for the more colourful costume. Was our production a mash-up of Bible story and Christmas dinner? Was I playing a *roast* carrot?

*

Overlooked and under-appreciated they may be, but I don't consider roots the poor relations of the vegetable world. I look forward to the colder months, not only because I dislike high temperatures and humidity, but because it's when root vegetables really come into their own.

Moroccan-spiced sweet potatoes.

Warm beetroot salad.

Latkes.

We tend to think of our own age as one of abundance and diversity but if you read the cookbooks and botanicals of yesteryear, it's evident that a much bigger range of vegetables was being grown and eaten. Many roots that were once mainstream have disappeared from our tables. Who now cooks with skirret or rampion? Serves up burdock or

Hamburg parsley?

Although— —

Soy-braised burdock root is a Korean staple.

And Hamburg parsley was an essential ingredient in my mother's chicken soup. In her borscht and baked dishes, too. A large-rooted variety of the familiar pot-herb, 'it looks like an under-privileged parsnip', according to Jane Grigson. It tastes like a nutty combination of celeriac and parsley leaves, and is popular in the cuisines of northern and central Europe. English greengrocers, at least those of the 1960s and '70s, didn't stock Hamburg parsley so Mum grew her own and gave the surplus to friends, like Mrs Krank – actually Mrs Krakowska but everyone called her Krank.

The last time I saw Mrs Krank she was living in a residential home for the elderly. I had a cup of tea with her and listened while she told me the same stories she told me as a child. About her grandfather's estate in southern Poland and endless prewar summers when shadows kept their distance and someone somewhere was always playing a Chopin mazurka.

'Nothing now is like the old days,' she sighed. 'Not even the weather.'

Her voice still had that slightly sad, faintly amused tone. The voice of exile.

'Memories are precious,' she told me. 'We have to treat them with care so they'll last out our lives.'

At the age of eight or nine Mrs Krank's reminiscences bored me silly; as an adult I feel as if I've wandered into a Chekhov play.

Outside are birch trees and frostbitten shrubs. Inside there's cherry compote and silver spoons.

I close my eyes and imagine a train travelling east from Moscow;

babushkas selling pickles;
the extraordinary nature of taken-for-granted things.

We were the children already lost from view
the sons and daughters who'd upped and left.

Families get scattered not only by dramatic events like war and migration, but also by routine decisions to travel, relocate for a job or seek affordable housing.

Migrating from England to Australia removed me from my past. I've spent a portion of the last couple of decades trying to – and this is a horrible word but I can't think how else to express it – narrativise it back to wholeness.

Social organiser and Harvard academic Marshall Ganz says we have to self-author our public story. If we don't, others will do it for us and we may not like the way they tell it. He also says that in a cosmopolitan world our roots are more than nationality, gender, religion or race. We're all part of what he calls 'multiple us's' – multiple constituencies and communities, those we've chosen as well as those we were born into.

*

We're rediscovering forgotten roots.

Thanks to concerns about sustainability, food miles and healthier diets, some of these forgotten roots are enjoying a revival. Purple carrots, Jerusalem artichokes, swedes, kohlrabi, unconventional roots, exotic roots, heirloom species and cultivars which may be slow growers or give smaller yields than supermarket high-performers.

*

Reunion has been a recurring theme on stage and screens. Think *Paris, Texas,* Ilsa and Rick in *Casablanca,* college friends coming together for a funeral in *The Big Chill*, the miraculous reunions of Shakespeare's *Pericles* and *The Winter's Tale*. In all of them there's an encounter between characters who haven't seen each other for years.

'Of all the gin joints in all the towns in all the world, she walks into mine.'

In our connected world, where just about everyone we've ever met can be tracked online, can you have a *Casablanca* moment? Experience the shock of coming face to face with a long-ago lover or running into your teenage nemesis now bald and beer-gutted.

And how does all this ready-made remembering affect our interior lives?

The man who walked out of the mist and into my Katoomba garden was – a total stranger.

There I was picking lilac when this old man appeared at the front gate.

'Dzień dobry Pani,' he said.

'Nie mówię po polsku,' I replied. I don't speak Polish.

He pulled a folded paper from his pocket. It was some kind of official document from a time before laminating and biometrics. When schools taught handwriting and awarded prizes for penmanship.

I didn't know what the document was – identity papers, some kind of passport? Proof that he was a refugee, a prisoner of war or simply a citizen of Warsaw or Gdansk?

The photo showed him young and dashing in military uniform. I remembered the Polish ex-airmen, the wartime aerodromes scattered through England, now sprouting weeds and development applications.

'I'm sorry, nie mówię po polsku,' I repeated.

His shirt was neatly ironed but the collar and cuffs

were fraying. And his disappointment was palpable. He hadn't found a compatriot or a fellow Polish speaker; he'd found me, London-born speaker of English, passable French, a little German and a smattering of Korean.

Had he scoured the phone directory for Polish surnames?

The playwright in me immediately started filling in a possible backstory. Wife: recently deceased. Children: interstate. Friends: yes, but no one left who shared his past or knew him as a young man. The loneliness that had him reading the phone book late into the night over a glass or a few of vodka. In a kitchen now empty of female presence. The single plate, knife, fork and one spoon washed up and draining in the rack. The loaf of bread that lasts a week.

He backed down the path towards the street. Apologising. A mistake, sorry to have bothered you. Sorry.

'Żegnaj Pani.'

I watched him trudge up the hill.

A few months later, I read in the local paper that an elderly man had been found dead in his home. Suicide could not be ruled out. The surname was Polish.

*

Have we outsourced memory to the clouds? To the continuous present of social media where nothing fades and nothing is ever forgotten? Until recently, as Viktor Mayer-Schönberger reminds us in *Delete: The Virtue of Forgetting in the Digital Age*:

'Remembering was hard and costly, and humans had to choose deliberately what to remember. The default was to forget. In the digital age…that balance of remembering and forgetting has become inverted.'

I imagine forests of family trees – massive canopies atop shallow roots.

We wonder about the lives pasted into old photo albums, about those we knew only briefly or from secondhand accounts. We wonder about the rootstock that leads to us, to here and now. So we start exploring, scrolling through websites and records on a quest for origins and explanations. Technology can put us in touch with our forebears; it takes only a mouse-click to unearth biographical details from the penumbra of the past. I've never researched a family history but I imagine there's a lot of conjecture involved. You run into gaps. You find your great-great-grandparents less glamorous than you'd hoped; neither courtesans nor revolutionaries, they were peasants, servants or blue-collar workers who left few lasting marks on the world.

Yet every life has its mysteries and surprises.

*

'The golden thistle, once growing, is a hardy plant...The flavour of its roots is, in our opinion, infinitely nicer than that of salsify and scorzonera...We cannot recommend its cultivation highly enough', wrote Pailleux and Bois.

I like salsify and scorzonera but I've never tried *Scolymus hispanicus*. What do its roots actually taste like?

'Very nice when properly cooked', said the *Adelaide Observer* of April 1882. Like oyster.

'It is described as having great delicacy of flavour', wrote the Reverend Professor G. Henslow. 'It is mentioned in some of our seed catalogues, Mr. Dickinson thus describing it: "This excellent vegetable is more productive and better flavoured than salsify...The roots are cooked and served like salsify."'

The Origin and History of our Garden Vegetables from 1912.

The previous year a widely syndicated article reported on

US government experiments with edible weeds and alien vegetables:

'The roots of the golden thistle have been found to be very delicious...Of course, cultivated varieties of this thistle are larger and better than the wild ones, but one may gather those found in pastures and meadows which are quite as nutritious. Thus, what has heretofore been regarded as a pest may now be looked upon as a partial blessing.'

The Bendigo Independent, Victoria, July 1911.

During World War II, as part of the 'Dig for Victory' campaign, the President of the English Wine and Food Society encouraged members to collect and cultivate wild plants, including golden thistles. When cooked, he said, these thistle roots tasted like tender parsnips.

Which brings me back to carrots— —

And Chekhov. Shortly before his death, the actor Olga Knipper Chekhova asked her husband about the meaning of life. That question, he replied, was like asking the meaning of a carrot. 'A carrot is a carrot and we know nothing more.'

THISTLE POTLUCK

'Thistle, *Carduus Mariæ*; our Lady's milky or dappled Thistle, disarmed of its Prickles and boiled, is worth Esteem…The young Stalks, about May, (and sold in our Herb-Markets) being peeled and soaked in Water, to extract the bitterness, boiled or raw, is a very wholesome Salad, eaten with Oil, Salt, and Pepper: some eat them sodden in proper Broth, or baked in Pies, like the Artichoke; but the tender Stalk boiled or fried some prefer; both nourishing and restorative.'

Acetaria: A Discourse of Sallets by John Evelyn, 1699.

I've translated seventeenth-century spellings into their contemporary forms for this recipe and for others of similar vintage.

*

'Lovely dish of thistles!

My item of free food is young milk-thistle leaves. Cut up like lettuce, with onion and apple added, it is a tasty salad dish. It is also good eaten in a sandwich with cheese.

$2 to Mrs Collins.'

The Australian Women's Weekly, December 1966.

Milk-thistle is a common name for several species but is most often applied to the variegated thistle (*Silybum marianum*). While you *could* eat its young leaves, I bet Mrs Collins was actually collecting sow thistles.

*

'Qirsa'nat Paste (Thistle jam)

Take a ratl [1 ratl = 469 grams] of thistle skin. Peel the

outer part of its irritants, and pound it well. Cook it in water to cover. Then add it to three ratls of honey, cleaned of its foam. Cook it until it takes the form of a paste.'

Hispanic-Maghreb Cooking during the Almohad Period, an anonymous thirteenth-century manuscript.

*

'To fricassee Artichoke-Bottoms for a Side-dish

Boil your Artichokes tender, take off the leaves and choke, when cold split every Bottom, dredging then with flour, and then dip them in beaten eggs, with some salt and grated nutmeg; then roll them in grated bread, fry them in butter; make gravy sauce thickened with butter, and pour under them.'

The Complete Housewife by Eliza Smith, 1727.

*

'Cure for Neuralgia…a poultice and tea made from our common field thistle. The leaves are macerated and used as a poultice on the parts affected, while a small quantity of the same is boiled down to the proportion of a quart to a pint, and a small wine glass of the decoction drank before each meal…God gave herbs for the healing of nations.'

The Home Cook Book of Chicago, 1874.

Compiled from recipes contributed by the ladies of Chicago and other cities. Published for the benefit of the Home for the Friendless.

How much is a quart?

How big were wine glasses in 1874?

*

'Thistle and Rock Melon…

Dig up the roots of the black or Scotch thistle, wash them,

and put them through a mincing machine, saving the juice until you have about half a kerosene-tinful of juice and root. Add to this one tin of Latimer's decoy, and one tin of poison. Any proprietary make, such as S.A.P. or Boska, will be suitable for this purpose. Mix the whole to the required consistency with pollard and bran, and sweeten with honey if obtainable. A tin is sufficient for a big day's poisoning.'

The Farmer and Settler, New South Wales, April 1927.

*

'Certain wild plants such as gundelia and Syrian thistle are prepared in the form of a stew or upside-down dishes...by putting half-cooked meat in a saucepan, slightly sautéed or fried vegetables are placed over it and soaked rice is put on the top. Water or broth is added. After cooking is completed, the mixture is turned upside down on a round serving dish with the meat on the top and the rice at the bottom.'

'The use of wild edible plants in the Jordanian diet' by S. K. Tukan, H. R. Takruri & D. M. Al-Eisawi, *International Journal of Food Sciences and Nutrition*, May 1998.

Everything simmers below the lid.

Recipes spill across borders. Migrate with the children. Evolve as ingredients become more or less available.

*

'Chardoons with Cheese

Cut them in bits an inch long, after they are stringed, then stove them in gravy till tender, season them with pepper and salt, and squeeze in an orange, thicken it with butter browned with flour. Put it in your dish, and cover it all over with Parmesan or Cheshire cheese, and then brown it up all over with a hot cheese iron, and serve it up.'

Primitive Cookery; or the Kitchen Garden Displayed, 1767.

No author credited, probably the work of multiple contributors.

No quantities, imperial or otherwise.

*

'Spear Thistle…

Few plants are more disregarded than this, and yet its use is very considerable…The flowers, like those of the Artichoke, have the property of Rennet in curdling milk.—— Sheep and swine refuse it; neither horses, cows, or goats are fond of it.—— The painted Lady Butterfly, *Papilio Cardui*, and the Thistle Ermine Moth, feed upon it.'

The Botanical Arrangement of all the Vegetables naturally growing in Great Britain by William Withering, 1776.

*

'Their use is always dangerous … and the taste which stock sometimes show for thistles in the fresh condition is a depraved one, like that of a man for drugs.'

The Weeds, Poison Plants, and Naturalized Aliens of Victoria by Alfred J. Ewart and J. R. Tovey, 1909.

*

'To Make a Sherdoon Pye in the Spring

There is a thistle which hath a root like an Artichoke, and must be boiled, and ordered accordingly: when it is boiled, you may season it with Cinnamon, Ginger, and beaten Nutmeg; you must take the marrow of four Marrow bones, season them with Cinnamon, Sugar, the yolks of three or four eggs, and grated bread. A thin coffin being ready, put in your Sherdoons, so wrap the marrow in the yolks of eggs, and put it into the pie, with a handful of Dates, and lay it on some sliced Lemmon, large Mace, put your Butter on, to close it, set it in the Oven: when it's enough, draw it [and] cut it up.'

The Whole Body of Cookery Distilled by William Rabisha, 1661.

Sherdoon is a variant spelling of cardoon.

Ditto chardoon with an h.

Nutmeg or mace – can you taste the difference?

*

'Tastier Than Jam.

Mr A. T. Howell, of Coolamon, has found that the roots of young black thistles cut into small pieces well washed and strained, powdered with strychnine and well stirred, is a more effective bait for rabbits than jam.'

The Sun, Sydney, August 1911.

*

'Cooked Thistles.—— are not much relished in England but in France are held in the highest estimation. Thistle is an entremet usually selected by a French chef to try the skill of a new cook. Chardons are delicious stewed with Spanish sauce, and mix well with poached eggs. They are perfect with beef marrow or with white and velouté sauce. The Spanish thistles are the best, being of the artichoke race. A French epicurean writer says, "this dish is the *ne plus ultra* of human science, and a cook who can cook thistles well is entitled to rank as the first artist in Europe"…Thistles *en malgre* and *au parmesan* are not difficult to cook and are extremely good. Persons of inferior genius should endeavor to acquire glory by first cooking their thistles in the humbler styles.'

The New York Times, January 1869.

An entremet used to be a palate cleanser or small dish served between courses. Now it's a layered mousse cake.

The same Alexandre Dumas who wrote *The Three*

255

Musketeers also wrote a *Grand dictionnaire de cuisine*. Over a thousand pages, it includes recipes for:

Spanish cardoons with marrow.

——au parmesan.

——with a ham glaze.

and cardoon ragoût.

*

'Thistle Salad for Hungry Berliners.

Epicures can now add thistle, nettle, dandelion, and wild vegetable salads to their tasty dishes list. Berliners are eating such foods every day and finding them to be quite good fare. They say all one needs is a trip into the woods, a mixing pot, and a good imagination…

The upper parts of the thistle should be cooked for at least 40 minutes…After cooking, put through the meat grinder, and then serve cold.

To achieve the supreme in tastiness one should mix together many wild vegetables…Place in a salad bowl, add a drop of vinegar, and you have the finest wild vegetable salad in post-war Germany.'

The Morning Bulletin, Rockhampton, Queensland, July 1947.

Same story in *The Singapore Free Press*—

and elsewhere.

EAT MORE THISTLES!

There are images that sear. Things you see that haunt you and go on haunting you years after the event. This is one of them. They're on their hands and knees. About twenty people, scrabbling around on a patch of bare earth. Some of them are wearing suits. Some are children with ragged hair and distended bellies.

Here's another image. Rice. Soup. Salad. Braised vegetables with hints of chicken. A square of white bread. Rancid butter. Beefsteak – extra well done. The meal is nothing to write home about but the setting is surreal. I'm the sole diner in this revolving restaurant on the forty-seventh floor of a Pyongyang hotel. It's 1.00 am. Outside is darkness, the only light the silent dancing of the stars.

I entered the Democratic People's Republic of Korea or DPRK one mid-October morning at the tail end of the 1990s. The train crossed the Yalu River that marks the border with China and pulled into Sinuiju, the first stop on the other side. Although crowded, the station concourse was oddly quiet. No chatter or scraping of bowls, no café muzak spilling into the ether – because, unless they were brilliantly disguised, the station was utterly devoid of food outlets.

From Sinuiju we clattered over a complication of tracks. Stopping frequently. Somewhere along the line we passed another train. A steam engine belching black smoke. It's gone midnight when I finally arrive in Pyongyang. After almost thirty hours of passive smoking and not so flush toilets, it's a relief to get off the train. Two guides and a driver whisk me to the hotel, where that well-done steak has been kept warm for me.

A slight exaggeration but, at the time of my visit, English books and internet sites about North Korea ran the gamut from N for nuclear to P for politics. Next to nothing about life behind the bluster. Where do people buy food? What makes them laugh? What do they like for breakfast?

I prod a scoop of scrambled egg and sip black tea – after last night's butter episode I've decided to forgo dairy for the duration.

This morning the view from the forty-seventh floor is panoramic.

This morning, Mr Kim, the younger of my two guides, asks if I want western or Korean meals. Foreigners, he says, often find the local cuisine too spicy. Not me. I grew up in Britain, enjoying the curries of the subcontinent.

After a tightly choreographed routine of monuments and hallowed shrines to the Great and Dear Leaders, I ask about the current famine. When the Soviet bloc ground to a halt so did its subsidised exports to North Korea. That loss coincided with disastrous floods. Supplies dwindled, farms and factories fell silent, the food distribution system collapsed. People began to starve.

Let's Eat Only Two Meals a Day!

Let's Tighten our Belts and Forward March!

Along with billboards promoting the less is better message, the regime urged its malnourished citizens to collect weeds, husks and tree bark. And mix those gleanings with regular ingredients to bulk out noodles or porridge. Consumption of these so-called substitute or alternative foods was portrayed as patriotic. The Central News Agency published stories reminding everyone that Kim Jong-il's own mother not only skipped meals but, when caring for a sick comrade, 'mounted rough ridges to pick the wild vegetables the patient liked to eat'.

As the famine progressed, recipes and field guides were issued in response to reports of digestive ailments and poisonings. Yet Korean cooks have a long history of harvesting and preparing wild food, and a wealth of knowledge about which plants are safe to eat and which are not. The ritual gathering of spring herbs and greens is celebrated in folk songs, verse and drama.

Choe In-hun's 1976 play *Away, Away, Long Time Ago* recognises their role as a survival food. 'All through the winter, wild greens and gruel...' A famished couple review their meagre rations. The husband coaxes his pregnant wife to supplement the greens with a portion of millet.

Reasons for the popularity of foraged vegetables include a surprisingly diverse native flora, the Buddhist belief that one should refrain from eating meat, and cycles of war and shortage.

'War is probably the single most powerful instrument of dietary change in human experience', wrote anthropologist Sidney Mintz.

*

The main thistle eaten both sides of the thirty-eighth parallel has no English name. In Korean it's *gondeure*. Its biological ID is *Cirsium setidens* and it's not your stereotypical thistle. It has the shaving-brush blooms but its leaves are soft-edged, not armed with prickles. Rich in nutrients, it grows abundantly in the mountainous areas which comprise about three-quarters of the Korean landmass and in spring, when the leaves and stems are tender, you can see it for sale in the markets of Seoul, Busan and elsewhere.

Pyeongchang in the northeast of South Korea hosts a Thistle Festival every May, when visitors can try local specialities featuring *C. setidens*, catch trout with their hands or compose a short, thistle-themed poem.

It was in South, not North, Korea that I sampled the country's thistles.

Mixed-up rice. That's the literal translation of the ubiquitous *bibimbap*. But Korean cuisine has a whole catalogue of dishes that combine rice with other grains, with legumes, with a specific vegetable or a selection. *Gondeure bap, --bibimbap* or *--namul bap* is seasoned thistle with rice. I ate it in restaurants made with either fresh thistles or leaves that had been dried for later use. But the time-poor home cook can buy a packet of *gondeure bap* in a just-add-water version – a bit like instant noodles.

The thistles have a clean, sharp taste, which is balanced with a few spoonfuls of soy-based dipping sauce.

Gondeure bap is one of those austerity recipes that's enjoying a revival as Koreans look to celebrate not only the culinary heritage of the Joseon Royal Court – labelled Important Intangible Cultural Asset Number 38 – but also good old-fashioned peasant know-how.

Back in the DPRK where the red star still flies high.

Kim Jong-il's epicurean indulgence was detailed in a cook-and-tell memoir by his erstwhile Japanese chef. While the Dear Leader scoffed caviar and crabmeat, the everyday people scavenged for stubble and scraps.

After a generous breakfast of *omeu raiseu*, that's omelette with rice, bean sprouts, sweet potatoes and a muddy yellow liquid that passes for fruit juice, we're off to Mount Myohyang. A place of scenic beauty, bracing temperatures and more obligatory honouring of the Kim dynasty.

More show.

More sham.

More vainglory.

The guidebook goes into the resort's gastronomic delights. Myohyangsan Wild Edible Greens, it declares, will be 'an unforgettable memory of an impressive experience for the tourists'.

For me it's another solitary meal in another hotel restaurant designed for mass gatherings. I wonder where the Taiwanese tour group and the large contingent of Japanese Koreans we met this morning are lunching. Not to mention my guides and driver: what are they eating in their separate staff canteen?

After lunch, a bushwalk. Unlike other regions where hillsides clear-felled for cultivation now suffer serious erosion, the slopes here are thickly wooded. At the foot of a waterfall, a brigade of artists, easels primed, paints the autumn colour.

'They are practising in nature,' explains my senior guide, Mr Pak.

I notice several picnic parties with lavish spreads of mandarins, grapes, zucchini, kimchi, beer and what looks like *bulgogi*. But something about it feels stage-managed. No one is tucking in. They're smiling and singing, and suddenly I'm pretty sure these merrymakers with their al fresco feast are performing plenty for the foreign tourists. This suspicion is supported when we cut short our hike and return to the picnic spot earlier than planned. To find the revellers packing up the untouched food.

Actual food may be scarce but displays of food are a consistent feature of life in the DPRK.

For weddings, those who can't afford the traditional banquet hire food from market vendors, take photos, then return the items.

Defectors tell of being given food before inspections by aid agencies and high-ranking cadres. Once the visitors went, so did the provisions.

And, of course, all those posters of happy, well-fed workers canning pears or clutching sheaves of wheat.

Dig Roots for the Revolution!

Let the Fragrance of the Big Fish Haul Permeate the Nation!

As well as slogans and visions of prosperity to come, there are musical tributes to staples like miso soup and radish kimchi. *Oh Ho Ho Potato Pride* is a jaunty number about a village elder who shares his allocation with the community. Check it out on YouTube.

But the fact is, no amount of nationalist razzle fills an empty stomach.

*

'The Korean is omnivorous', reported Isabella Bird from the outer reaches of colonial adventure. They consume 'wild leaves and roots innumerable'.

Namul is the collective term for seasoned vegetables commonly served as accompaniments to the main event. Horticulture supplies the bulk but wild plants – many of which lack an English rendition – are also widely used. Some side-dish vegetables are left raw but thistles are invariably cooked. Temple fare is the apex of *namul* cuisine and, seeking shelter one rainy day near the Jongmyo Shrine area of Seoul, that's where I observed this process.

Thistle leaves were blanched. Excess water squeezed out. A little salt added, a drizzle of sesame oil and a pinch of toasted seeds to finish.

The North Korean menu has a discernible Russian flavour,

according to some commentators. I can see similarities between the tastes of Korea and Eastern Europe: a fondness for preserved and fermented produce, for cabbage and mushrooms in all their delicious diversity.

Let Us Turn Ours into a Country of Mushrooms!

In Poland the leaves of several thistle species were boiled or fried and eaten with potatoes or a splash of milk. A makeshift food for hard times.

I imagine bees poking into thistle heads, waysides rowdy with grasses and pollen.

I imagine Soviet-style dystopias, featureless concrete and searchlights so fierce they blind the stars.

When Yugoslavia broke apart it created a food crisis, something not experienced in the West since World War II. During the siege of Sarajevo in the early 1990s Bosnian botanist Sulejman Redžić documented the use of emergency biota (including Scotch and sow thistles) and ran programs explaining how to recognise and cook a range of plants generally dismissed as weeds. Before the conflict, the inhabitants knew next to nothing about the many palatable species growing rough on their doorstep. But they learnt fast and those wildings helped avert nutritional catastrophe.

*

Cold buckwheat noodles: Pyongyang's signature dish. Tonight I'm joined by my entourage in a restaurant patronised by Party heavyweights and individuals with overseas currency. While the courses come and go, a band plays tunes from the DPRK top ten. Not that North Korea has a hit list – at least not for music. The cuisine here is sophisticated, sour and sweet, tangy and delicate, but it leaves a bitter taste in my mouth. I'm feasting in a land of famine.

Statistics don't tell the story on a human scale. Nor does

polemic or positioning North Korea as an ideological dinosaur. How do people get by? Make sense of their difficulties? What fills the gap between government bombast and reality?

'Mr Pak has overdrunk,' announces Mr Kim the following morning. He'll join us later.

It was either the Ragwon Department Store or the Number One Department Store – I can't remember which. But I do remember bottles of blueberry wine, Chinese imports and honey from Bulgaria. More presentations of food out of reach for all but the elite.

So where do the rank and file shop for food? When I question Mr Kim about markets, he tells me they don't exist except for agricultural stuff. No foreigners allowed. But there *are* improvised markets. I've caught glimpses of them from the car window.

On the road to Kaesong and the Demilitarised Zone that splits the peninsula, there's hardly any traffic. Just the occasional tank or ox-cart. Signs of life are few and far between. Here a cluster of houses, roofs covered in squash vines. There that group of people on their hands and knees combing the dirt for anything remotely edible. Skinny figures who look as if they've been sandpapered close to the bone by hunger and circumstance.

Have I ever been hungry enough to eat the face of a daisy? Chew on a wood chip? No, I haven't. I can't even imagine that kind of hungry. Not really.

Whenever I bring up the famine, both guides stick to their Cold War guns and insist it's a temporary shortfall caused by a confluence of environmental and imperialist forces.

What carrots and sticks sustain this state-directed

amnesia? Persuade people to rewrite or relinquish their memories?

In the hunt for edible weeds, thistles would be prime pickings. *Cirsium setidens* is a perennial. By now thistles growing here would have flowered and gone to fluff. Leaving stalks, foliage and the spent flower heads to wither before they die back completely during winter. But nowhere in North Korea do I see the shrivelled remains of a single thistle.

*

For a writer or researcher the DPRK presents challenges. The only time you're unaccompanied is when you go to sleep at night. The only sights you see are authorised. The only narrative is the official script. There are subtexts no one will voice.

What you do hear are slogans. Slogans and more slogans.

February 2015, North Korea released its latest crop. Over three hundred new slogans. A list peppered with exclamation marks. Sentences whose tone ranged from exhortation to threat to the strangely poetic.

Let Us Build a Fairyland for the People by Dint of Science!

Let Us Resolutely Frustrate the Anti-DPRK 'Human Rights' Schemes by the US and its Puppets!

Make Fruits Cascade Down and Their Sweet Aroma Fill the Air on the Sea of Apple Trees at the Foot of Chol Pass!

What I want to know is who writes them? A committee of Party-approved scribes, no doubt. As I speculated – could *I* get work penning slogans? – I decided to play around with them and invent a few of my own. Let's start with –

Eat More Thistles!

There are no menus in the hotel restaurants where I take my meals. And therefore no possibility of impromptu grazing or making an on-the-spot choice. On the bright side, however, because I've opted for Korean I'm spared that pan-western fare beloved of hotels the world over.

Let's Call it Tourist Food!

Mid-Pacific pizzas, Russian salads lost in translation.

Both sides tilt history their own way. Today clouds hang low and grey, and I'm the only visitor on the Northern side of this heavily fortified corridor that divides the DPRK from its Southern twin. The first time I was here I stood on the other side, part of a day trip from Seoul. It was 1993 and in the mess or dining facility or whatever the American army called it, I had my worst ever meal in Korea. Reconstituted potato. Fried luncheon meat. Processed cheese. Tomatoes drowned in syrupy mayonnaise. Beans with the bite boiled out of them. A dessert confection straight from the chemistry lab.

Jjigae is one of my favourite Korean dishes. Hearty stews of various types. Tofu *jjigae*. Seafood *jjigae*. Not forgetting that epitome of fusion food, GI *jjigae,* or military camp stew.

'To many Westerners the name Korea is apt to suggest far-flung battlefronts...rather than the unequivocal pleasures of the table.' So opens Harriet Morris's *The Art of Korean Cooking* published in 1959, just six years after the end of the Korean War. Created in the wake of that war, GI or military camp stew is a spicy hodgepodge of manufactured meats like Spam and hot dog sausages, ramen noodles, macaroni, kimchi, vegetables and any other leftovers impoverished Koreans could scrounge from US military bases. It's not quite as disgusting as it sounds and it's become a favourite with a young generation unfamiliar with its provenance.

The stall is Bomchae Bibimbap or Mixed Rice. The dish is *gondeure bibimbap,* or seasoned thistle with rice.

December 2016, a couple of days before Christmas. I'm eating *gondeure bibimbap*, not in the quietude of a temple restaurant, but in the noisy food court of the Lotte Department Store in downtown Seoul. It's midday and already there are queues of shoppers, students and workers on their lunch breaks.

It's over a decade since I was last in Korea and a lot has changed. For one thing, smoking is no longer permitted in cafés and eateries. Yay!

The Lotte food court has bakeries with French- and Italian-sounding names, Japanese *katsu* counters, a stall where they make complicated sandwiches, and much, much more, but it's thistle rice for me.

Outside the mercury hovers around zero degrees.

I assume the thistles are frozen.

There's more food and more variety of food available in North Korea today than there was when I visited. Italian has entered the scene with spaghetti and pizzas given an indigenous twist with kimchi and chilli paste. Due in part to the influence of illegal South Korean TV, eating out has become fashionable for city dwellers who can afford it. The state runs cooking contests and a recipe website aimed at housewives – their term not mine. Pyongyang now has street vendors, markets selling snacks, kitchen basics, even pineapples and other exotic goods for the rich or well connected. These shifts have been driven not so much by the big shots at the top of the political pyramid, but by the desperation and resourcefulness of ordinary subjects.

'It seems that anything can happen when it's hard for people to survive', says one of the characters in *Away, Away, Long Time Ago*.

Available literature about North Korea has also expanded

to include novels, genre fiction and, of course, defectors' dramatic tales of escape to the West – or, more accurately, the South. Stories that often struggle to carry the heft of exile with all its attendant turmoil and melancholy.

Onion pancake. Fish in a piquant broth. Lettuce, bean paste, rice and an array of side dishes. My last supper in Pyongyang is very yum. Afterwards I stand in the hotel car park to drink in the night sky with its mighty acreage of stars. Power restrictions mean light pollution is minimal. A bonus for those of us just passing through. A deficit for the citizens of this unfortunate country.

Let's All Hope for Change!

OUTLIERS

THE BOOK OF THISTLES

AFRICAN THISTLE

I didn't choose to come here, you know. But yeah, I'm into sand – coastal by nature. Bunch of us hung out near the harbour. Doing whatever to scratch an existence. There was uncertainty. A state of terror. There was a boat.

Answer all questions.[3] Name: *Berkheya rigida*. Otherwise known as: African thistle. Evidence of identity: The genus *Berkheya* was named after the eighteenth-century Dutch naturalist, poet and polemicist Johannes le Francq van Berkhey. Country of origin: South Africa. Date of arrival in Australia: 1906. Describe how you arranged to leave illegally: As seed in ballast dumped by ships when they docked at Australian ports – probably. Status in this country? What happened to your documents? Any past or present links? Yes. No. Other – give details. My head becomes a burr – or do I mean a blur? So many questions.

Background information. All biological relatives, living, deceased or whereabouts unknown. The Asteraceae, yes, sometimes called Compositae or daisy, is a very large family. And widespread. Branches pretty much everywhere except Antarctica. Character: Individual African thistles are on the short side. Stems are stiff. Flowers are yellow. Reproduction: Vegetative and sexual. Risk to national security: Underground

---

3   The questions are loosely adapted from the Australian Government Department of Immigration and Border Protection Form 842. Application for a Refugee and Humanitarian visa.

activity. Potential environmental weed. May form self-sustaining monocultures. Colonies of *Berkheya rigida* spread from rhizome regrowth. And when stems fall over, touch the earth and take root.

Barbed wire under bougainvillea blossom. Into old rhythms come new words. List all the jobs held in the last fifteen years. Look, if I smell beer-soaked, it's an accident – a drunken idiot lost his bottle. But I've been cheek by leaf with Shakespeare, Nadine Gordimer, ads for Viagra. And Sherlock Holmes. The product of living in a tip. A mountain of books and paper waiting to be recycled. Pulp. Hardbacks bursting at the seams. Skinny monographs. Travel guides to places that no longer exist. Forgotten conference proceedings. The occasional manuscript smuggled out.

GLOBE THISTLES

It's all about the drama with this one. *Echinops*. A genus of some hundred-plus species known collectively as globe thistles. The name comes from the Greek word for hedgehog and the story, like so many thistle stories, comes from the sunny, stony landscapes of Eurasia. A weed – not so much. Its primary narrative is that of a garden plant.

Atop each stem sits a firework of a bloom, a spherical inflorescence if you want to get technical about it. Depending on the species and/or cultivar, these cover the spectrum from the palest mauvy-grey to a deep cobalt.

'Hardy plants of large growth and suitable for certain kinds of gardens. They are too rank growers for moderate sized gardens. Valuable for producing sub-tropical effects.'
The Jewell Nursery Co, Minnesota, 1908.

A stately perennial.
Big plants for background.
Handsome in the herbaceous border.
That's how seed catalogues and horticultural literature of the early twentieth century described *Echinops*.

A bold statement, a living sculpture, its architectural qualities prized by gardeners. Likewise its tolerant nature and its ability to attract clouds of pollinators, especially butterflies and bees. A bit more archival truffling tells me that the globe thistle was sometimes known as the honey plant.

In the 1880s the introduction of the Chapman honey plant (*Echinops sphaerocephalus*) from France generated excitement among apiarists on both sides of the Atlantic, with reports of bee visits (to the globe thistle blooms) on an almost unprecedented scale. Ultimately, however, the great expectations weren't realised. This is from the December 1918 edition of *Gleanings in Bee Culture*:

'I never saw bees so thick upon any other honey plant. But close observation showed that the bees were not in eager haste in their usual way when getting a big yield, but were in large part idle, and it looked a little as if the plant had some sort of stupefying effect upon them.'

September and the flowerbeds in the Oxford Botanic Garden offer a rainbow of opportunity for photographers and insects. Unlike most of the Garden's human visitors, flitting around as the fancy takes us, the bees are flying to a plan. They're bypassing orange and yellow flowers and heading straight for the blues. Is that where the term 'beeline' comes from?

With one or two exceptions, the names of the species/cultivars read like variations on a theme:
Blue glow
Arctic glow
Star frost
Platinum blue
Veitch's blue
Taplow blue
Taplow purple
Blue pearl
Blue cloud
Sea stone
Moonstone
Charlotte and The Giant.

'Tall and showy plants, like the tallest girls in the ballet, are usually given a back place in the garden. There are dozens of these tall growers, mostly perennials, to make a wonderful display of colour…Globe thistles, or echinops, are decorative spiny plants which grow easily from seed sown in spring or autumn and produce blue flowers on 3ft. stems lasting many weeks.'

The Australian Women's Weekly, November 1962.

Enter stage left…

I once had a short-lived job as Artistic Director of a community theatre in Melbourne. It was a difficult time for many reasons, not least because I was only a couple of months off the plane from England. And although the interview panel said they wanted my new broom and fresh ideas, the incumbent staff clearly didn't. We soon parted ways and I swept the whole miserable experience into the crappy-history-best-forgotten bin. But I've held on to the memory of one company member delivering a ridiculous tirade about 'middle-class trees' – blue gums, blue spruce and others with foliage in the blue-grey range.

He wasn't alone in his analysis. While plants per se are not part of the class system, a person's choice of flowers apparently speaks volumes about their social status.

Lady Kitty (obviously a pen name) wrote: 'Nature is far less prodigal of blue in plants than of yellow, red, white, or rose. That may be the reason why flowers of pure blue are usually so grateful to the eye.'

Saturday Journal, Adelaide, August 1923.

Nine years earlier a Canadian newspaper lauded the 'indisputable superiority' of blue flowers:

'Botanists will tell us that those plants which have reached the stage of plant life where they are capable of producing blue blossoms, have reached the highest known stage of plant development.'

The article continued its riff on the virtues – or not – of blueness. To be labelled a bluestocking is frightful, but to have blue blood in your veins 'pre-supposes a development, physically and morally and mentally, from the most exclusive and most enduring stock that obtains'.

The Toronto World, August 1914.

Despite their colour, globe thistles didn't always make the posh list. 'Rather coarse flowers which cannot be classed with some of the daintier or more refined flowers', was the verdict of the *Southeast Missourian*'s gardening columnist in July 1956.

Undemanding.

Requires no pampering.

The foliage doesn't bite.

Those are its positive features.

I can't remember where I read this but, as someone who likes lower-pitched instruments, such as the cello and bass clarinet, I liked the analogy: a lack of blue-flowering plants in a garden is akin to a musical composition without a bass part.

If there were more true-blue species would we value them less? Does the price we put on scarcity blind us to the beauty and worth of the ordinary?

Trends in gardening and design come and go. Some arrive with fuss and fanfare only to fade away. Others influence thinking for years to come.

'Blue as a colour is of the greatest value in a landscape

and, with white, identifies the discriminating gardener. If you watch a novice selecting plants the first choice is usually flaming red, followed closely by orange and yellow. As the spectrum runs from hot to cold, so experienced gardeners display their cool sophistication.'

Canberra Times, October 1984.

Hot colours were common, white and blue flowers were classy. Gardening advice of the 1980s was unequivocal on the matter. Ah yes, the 1980s...

The decade that's been spliced and repackaged for popular consumption and nostalgia marketing bears scant relation to the years I lived through, first as a postgrad student at the London School of Economics and Political Science (before its degrees became passports to careers in banking and international finance) and later as an arts worker. Things we shunned or satirised like royal weddings, huge shoulder pads and Band Aid's *Do They Know It's Christmas?* have somehow become the period's iconic markers.

I was seven-and-a-half years on this side of the globe before I made my first trip back to England. To Goff's Oak, where I grew up, and where my parents still lived. The nowhereness of the place was overwhelming. The streets are modern, but pleasant modern. Semi-detached houses with leadlight details and concrete paving fashioned to resemble flagstone. The kind of streets politicians have in mind when they talk about hard-working average families. A street for school teachers, locksmiths and middle managers married to nurses.

There was Mrs Newman who'd had 'her insides removed', Mrs Wallace who went into hospital with 'nerves' and came out with part of her brain removed, and Eileen Mac forever telling us we'd 'grow out of it' – whatever 'it' was.

*

'These plants are for naturalisation in wild gardens and shrubbery', suggests a nursery catalogue from 1908. Which begs the question: are globe thistles ornamentals or weeds? Although imported for home backyards and farmed for the cut-flower trade, they have frequently spread to roadsides, fence lines and edgelands. The majority of gardening forums insist they're not aggressive and won't become a pest. Well, assurances blah-blah, the fact is *Echinops sphaerocephalus* is sometimes cultivated and sometimes escapes from cultivation. *The Introduced Flora of Australia and its Weed Status* (2007) records seventeen introduced *Echinops* species, with *E. sphaerocephalus* a certified escapee. It's judged a weed in parts of North America. Also in New South Wales, where it grows in the central-west of the state, and 'is considered likely to expand from its current limited distribution'. *Weeds of the South-East* by F. J. Richardson, R. G. Richardson and R. C. H. Shepherd, 2011.

In other words, the globe thistle is a potential sleeper weed.

February 2004, I had the world in my hands. Vienna's Globe Museum is open to visitors for a single hour twice a week, and I've snagged one of those slots. There's a worldview from seventeenth-century Amsterdam and a small world on a stand, metal arm attached to the North Pole, that takes me back to an empty classroom and the mud-spattered geography of childhood.

Globes represent the earth and sometimes the firmament. They're at once scientific instruments and art objects. Paper maps flatten the world. A sphere presents the undistorted planet, proportional reproductions of continents, oceans, stars beckoning infinity.

Time's up! The Museum is closing. I leave the earth turning on its axis, the past defying its own gravity.

*

Echinops is often linked with another genus of similar design appeal: *Eryngium* or sea holly. The two genera share some characteristics – a spiky aspect and flowers of metallic iridescence, for example – but *Eryngium* isn't part of the daisy mob. It's a member of the Apiaceae, a family of more than two hundred species scattered around the world.

Blue devil (*Eryngium ovinum*) is an Australian native with vaguely threatening foliage, steely blue flowers and, according to some botanical websites, unexploited potential as a garden or rockery plant.

Giant sea holly (*Eryngium giganteum*) also goes by the name Miss Willmott's ghost, after the Edwardian plantswoman Ellen Ann Willmott's (alleged) habit of carrying its seeds in her pocket and surreptitiously sowing them in other people's gardens. Whether this covert propagation of the silvery thistle-headed species was an act of munificence or mischief is open to debate.

Despite that seed-sprinkling fairytale, Ellen Willmott was no batty old maid. She created spectacular gardens; she travelled and collected plants in Europe and sponsored plant-hunting expeditions to more distant lands; she wrote, developed photographs in her own darkroom, played the violin and sang in the Bach Choir.

In 1875 the teenage Ellen moved with her family to a country estate near Brentwood in Essex. (Brentwood is twenty-odd miles east of Goff's Oak and thirty from central London. In 1875 it was a rural parish. Today it's part of the same dreary, outer suburban hinterland as Goff's Oak.)

An inheritance from her godmother gave Ellen the fortune

and the freedom to pursue her passion for plants. And no way was she going to settle for a back-row seat. She stormed the male preserves of the Royal Horticultural Society and its Narcissus Committee, and in 1905 was one of the first women to be elected a fellow of the Linnean Society.

Ellen's life was rags to riches in reverse. For reasons both predictable and happenstance, the money ran out. The honours of her last decade were eclipsed by financial troubles and a 1928 shoplifting charge.

Nature has since reclaimed the grounds of the Essex house but the property is still haunted by Miss Willmott's ghost. Among the jumble of local flora, the Caucasian native, her trademark *Eryngium giganteum,* continues to self-seed and shoot anew each year.

I like sea holly and buy bunches whenever I see it for sale in markets or florists. And I like prickly, persistent Ellen Ann Willmott. Without her story, horticulture would be a less interesting field.

And I like globe thistles. Resilient individualists whose flowers look like pincushions, whose seeds ride the wind.

THISTLE NOIR

You know the score: early Miles or Lester Young in all his
(subtle) harmonic glory. Classic blues in black and white.

Thistles live in the details
in the tense present and the past
among the daisies
and in cracks
around buildings of civic pride.

Theirs is the car park and wasteland
the ripped poetry
the pissy underside.
It's the plant that shoots first,
the scratch on your hand.
It's the plant that survives
and helped Aunty Mara survive the war.

Thistles live in the details
in countries that never asked to have them
or thanked them for coming
and staying
and making themselves at home.

*

Scene 2. Consider the clues:
Rain, reflection, random carnage.
On the (Persian) carpet – a layout of thistles.

No parlourmaid, no ingénue,
no eccentric aunt to pick out a pattern.
Instead, a hard-boiled Inspector
encounters a promiscuous flora fatale.

Background check throws up a swag of aliases:
Black thistle, bank thistle, boar and bull,
swamp, green, common, plume,
spear and more.
Officially *Cirsium vulgare*, previously *lanceolatum*,
that's where the spear came in.

Weedkillers in the shed
knives and machete there for the taking.
Small wonder the case remains unsolved.

The soundtrack shifts: something jagged, asymmetrical, late
Coltrane or Pharaoh Sanders. Music for wild thoughts.
Known associates:
honey bees, various Lepidoptera,
small birds, goats, sometimes mules.

The flower bases are grenade-shaped
and razor-wired.
It's typical, it's textbook,
it's the thistle you see in your mind's eye
when you hear the word.

Voiceover:
A thistle is a thistle in anybody's language, and they had
trouble written all over them. We didn't know much back
then. But we knew about weeds and we wanted them the

hell out. It was the first time we'd seen an Inspector issue a photofit. Has anyone seen this plant? It's dangerous. The wildest of the wild. If you see it, contact…

*

Flashback:
Spear thistles have spread far and wide from their European and west Asian homelands – to Pacific islands, the Americas, temperate east Africa, pretty much everywhere. They came to Australia in the wake of European settlement, and they arrived early. Hobart newspapers of the 1830s mentioned their ruderal nature and insolent vitality. Mentioned forests of thistles springing up on vacant ground and amassing in the back streets like a gang of conspirators. Although *Cirsium vulgare* wasn't explicitly identified, pound to a penny it was a major offender.

*

Impro:
Privet hedge, poached eggs, Ted Hughes
grinds words together in splendid ways.
The ultimate *Thistles* (poem)
remembered far beyond schoolbook English
'every one a revengeful burst'.
The fish in the glass case is stuffed.
Paper bags, ivy-clad, John Clare
wrote with homemade ink.
His *Spear Thistle* spurred with thorns is a thing
'not undevoid of beauty'.
To jazz is to loiter
a collection of notes
about going somewhere and coming home.

THE ILLUSTRATED THISTLE

LOTTE
This is what happened. I got the aliens.
My first up-close encounter
with *Carduus nutans*.

Scalpel.

Magnifying glass.

Loose sheets.
Pencils. Graphite. 3H to 6B.
Triple zero paintbrush – check.

For all the advances in photography, the camera still falls
short.
Science needs the human hand.
A pen and ink portrait,
a botanical illustration lets you ask different questions
opens up perennial problems in new ways – maybe.
Definitely. Sometimes.

Tweezers.

Scissors. Surgical. Cutting edge.

I work only with live specimens.

In the field I film the plant in situ,

THE BOOK OF THISTLES

note habitat, the fall and dapple of sunlight on its leaves,
shadows growing long and delicious –
Outside the field
you need to cultivate a good grower.
I've got Mitch, actually Mitchell, but he prefers the sawn-off
version. He talks like that, too, in sawn-off sentences.
Water. Duck's back. Paddle on.

My name is L-O-double T-E and that E-at-the-end is
pronounced as an A. Lotte as in lotta attitude.
Surname Martens – Dutch in case you're wondering.
Small damp country, lotta people. Horizon flat as a spirit-
level.
You can see a long way, like Australia, but that doesn't mean
things are out in the open. Also like Australia.

OK. This is what happened. I chose the aliens.
Everyone's doing rare or endangered,
everyone else has gone native,
so I thought: I'll do the ring-ins.
I chose this one for its big head:
Carduus nutans. The nodding or musk thistle
has the largest flower head of any thistle. Four to eight
centimetres across, including bracts. Bracts, by the way, are
modified leaves from the area just below the flower.
You have to know your way around a plant to make this kind
of art.
Study the junctions,
how leaves attach to the stem,
the way its hefty crimson-purple blooms nod over, and
measure the angle of their droop.
But the nodding thistle discourages intimacy. It's covered –
leaves, stems, almost entirely – in spines.

I handle it with kid-leather gloves and position it with tongs,
but still, somehow, it gets to me
and I collect a few puncture wounds.

Dig out the First Aid box with its disinfectant smell.

Black and white is economical,
keeps the lid on printing costs for academic books and
journals.
Designed to help botanists ID different species.
But ink is unforgiving.

Clamp.

Cloth.

Watercolours – check.
Coloured pencils – five hundred plus.
They're my preferred medium. I love their transparency and
forgiving nature.
Keep sharp with a quick hit
into the electric sharpener.
Then superfine sandpaper
if you need to emphasise the point.

Look. This is what happened.
We're not talking about ladies who dabbled,
a spot of water-colouring
between the embroidery and Earl Grey.
We're talking about a tremendous contribution to scientific
discovery
made by women serious about their art – and their science.

Botanical art evolved
in tandem with technologies
that allowed us to see more of the natural world, and in more
detail.
Think microscopes.
Think curiosities from exotic climes and a public hungry
for pictures.
Come the eighteenth century
combinations of words and images were the norm,
and much – no, maybe most – of this botanical art was
created by women.
Excluded from universities and learned societies,
their work dismissed as drawing-room botany.[4]
Yet beyond these closed doors
women acquired substantial scientific knowledge –
all the while practising
what appeared to be the dainty feminine art of painting
flowers.
But get this – a lot of these women took up *flora illustrata*
to pay off their husbands' debts and keep the lousy bastards
out of prison.

Paper. Hot-pressed.
Make a mark.
The golden rule of greens is to layer the shades.

There's a species of tropical chestnut with flowers enlarged.

---

4 *Drawing-Room Botany* by James H. Fennell was published in 1840.
'Its object is to enable Ladies (for whom it is principally written)...
to determine the class to which any flower belongs, by reference to the
annexed system, and the plates by which it is illustrated.' These plates were
created by Mrs E. E. Perkins.

There's a montage of rambutan luminous and full of mystery.
There's a pericarp, a petal, a poinciana,
specifics to be learnt rather than consumed.
When Berthe Hoola van Nooten's husband died in 1847 he
left her his debts – and a young family to bring up alone.
To make ends meet she produced watercolour plates of
plants from Java, where she was then living. *Fleurs, fruits
et feuillages choisis de l'ile de Java (The Fruits and Flowers of
Java)* was published in 1863–64.
We know sweet F-all about Madame Hoola van Nooten.
But we do know that she died in poverty in Batavia (now
Jakarta) at the age of seventy-four. And we know that, when
fellow botanical artist Marianne North visited her in Java, she
was struck by the Dutchwoman's straitened circumstances.

Bitter fruits.
Still life.
Citrus zingy as Cézanne's.
Apple cart. Upset.
You know how it goes –
To cut themselves a slice
of the male-controlled pie
women went down the only professional paths open to them:
illustrators, assistants, gardeners, collectors, writers on things
horticultural.

Dissecting knife.

I'm invading
their privacy
probing with pencil point
to discover thistle secrets
casings, pappus bristles, sticky pollen, seeds the wind spins

away or doesn't.
One nodding thistle flower produces hundreds of seeds,
a single plant thousands.
That's a lotta seeds.
Vernalisation is botanic vocab for chilling,
and for this thistle to flower,
vernalisation in the rosette stage is a must.
Because of that low temperature requirement, nodding
thistles are pretty much confined to cool temperate areas.
In Australia they're found on the New South Wales tablelands,
in parts of Victoria and Tasmania.
Mitch – my grower, remember him? – told me there's a
close-related species that occurs sporadically in southeast
Queensland.
I looked it up
it's called *Carduus thoermeri*
and it's not a weed.

Mitch has hair like potato peelings
and the kind of body that's out of place in an office.
He doesn't sit down
he shovels himself into chairs
like a spade into the soil of his grandparents' farm.

Like I said, I draw from life
and the life of a plant once picked is short –
So Mitch is growing some. Nodding thistles. Extras. For me.
See, I've picked up his chop-chop syntax.

This is my first time
with a thistle – professionally speaking.
I'm cutting it to examine the structures that lie
beneath the surface.

Outside the studio, the sky is dark (Gunmetal with a smudge of Burnt Sienna) and full of rain.

Did I sketch and paint as a kid?
I don't know...
I got sick in my teens, so I've got a story about my past more than actual memories of it –
Though perhaps we all do that? Get through childhood then reconstruct it as adults to fit our self-image.
It was my psych, Dr Rikmans-call-me-Alex, who suggested art therapy.
I was running wild, drawing would keep me in line.
I'll say this for him, Dr Rikmans was an efficient man. I found him a bit of a tickbox, but that's me.

Keep your sense of scale.
Life-size as a rule,
although you may want to magnify some of the details.

Nodding thistles bolt when you're not looking.
They're brash and competitive, they break through
and crack up
on pasture and prairie.

This is what happened. Nodding thistles were introduced into North America in the early–mid nineteenth century, initially in ships' ballasts, later in seed stock.
Outside its homeland (north Africa, Asia Minor and Europe as far afield as Siberia) the species has a reputation as a serious weed.
Nodding thistle is a relatively recent arrival in Australia. And same as it did in the United States, Canada and Argentina, it came uninvited. The earliest reliable record is July 1950 from

a paddock at Oberon in New South Wales, and the plant was most likely present for several years before it was identified. Identified with the aid of accurate, hand-drawn illustrations – can't prove that of course, but I bet it was.

Before it came here, it was there— —
Nodding thistles had already made themselves at home in New Zealand.
The plant was documented by Thomas Kirk in *The Students' Flora of New Zealand and the Outlying Islands* (1899). He called it 'Musky thistle' – yes, the flowers do have a sweet, faintly sweaty smell.
It's since spread to become a major agricultural weed, and that's how it got to Australia,
a contaminant in pea seed imported from New Zealand.

Nodding thistledown was once used as a material to make paper.

Paper matters.

Likewise erasers – putty, plastic. Selection of.

We don't know how to fit
first-person perspectives
into the third-person world
of science,
so we remove them.

You read up on nodding thistles and it's all about how to get rid of them.

If we could eliminate mosquitoes – go for it.

With plants I'm live and let live— —
Though there's a few I think are overexposed.
Here's my top four dislikes:
Carnations fattened overseas.
Water lilies – forever trying to live up to the artist's impression.
Forsythia – it screams corporate landscaping.
Weeping anything except willows.

Nodding thistles are your basic thistle, the kind eaten by
Eeyore (from *Winnie the Pooh*) and spat out by Tigger who
'…doesn't like honey and haycorns and thistle
Because of the taste and because of the bristles.'
Nodding thistles are pithy, and I'll take pith over elegance
any day.

Sessions with Dr Rikmans and other psychs often ended
with them making suggestions:
'You'll be more comfortable, Lotte, if we adjust your
medication.'
Yeah right. They wanted to increase the dose of whatever I
was on to make themselves feel more comfortable.

When I walked down hospital corridors with Dr Rikmans I'd
stay deliberately out of step with him.
I still do that
with anyone.
I want my feet to make their own individual prints.

Outside the rain has stepped up.
It's rain Dutch-style, weltering, guttering downpipes.
There, it gushes underground where drains empty into
sluices and sluices discharge into the North Sea.
Here, it comes after a run of unbearably hot days followed by

equally uncomfortable nights.
I suspect it won't be enough to clear the air.

It's not about emotion; it's about translating the world
of botany.
The way we think about emotion is too narrow, too obvious.
To love and hate and all the usual suspects, I'd like to add
curiosity.
And I'm in good company –
Darwin believed curiosity was an emotion.

Have you ever really looked at a thistle?
Take off the 'invasive' and 'shouldn't be here' glasses,
turn on curiosity and, wow, thistle design is amazing.

Hold that thought.

And take a closer look the next time you notice a thistle.

THISTLY MARSH

I discovered Thistly Marsh in 2009. I was in England for the first anniversary of my father's death. And I was struggling, not only with my own and my mother's grief but also with feelings of restlessness and anxiety. Staying in my parents' house, sleeping in my teenage bedroom, my Australian life seemed remote. Chimerical. I was sinking. I needed something to hang on to, I needed solid ground. I went looking for it – and found Thistly Marsh.

*

How are marshlands formed? Provide examples and sketch maps where possible.

Southeast Hertfordshire is a watery place. The River Lea rises in the Chiltern Hills and empties into the Thames at Bow Creek. Along its course it's pierced by tributaries, canals, millstreams, cuts and flood-relief channels. On the map Thistly Marsh is a dance of small print and symbols among the ponds, wetlands and factories that characterise the lower reaches of the Lea Valley.

I went to Thistly Marsh because of its name, and because it was nearby. In 2009 I borrowed my mother's car and drove there. Later visits I caught the bus from Goff's Oak to Cheshunt Station. Over the level crossing, turn right and there it is: Thistly Marsh. Part of the Lea Valley Regional Park.

A floodplain of memories.

The outdoor swimming pool, scene of adolescent flirtations and secret smoking. The filled-in gravel pits where we had scuba diving lessons. The night we took acid and cruised around this Hazchem part of town. We turned up the volume on the car radio. Early Patti Smith and contaminants laced the air as we tripped and hopscotched over weed-cracked asphalt and sticky tar seams.

The pool has been demolished but the quarry lakes are still a feature. Over Hall Marsh Scrape a flock of birds flies in winding spirals as though pushed into shape by a council leaf-blower.

List the activities taking place in and around the Marsh; e.g., recreation, entomology, vehicle maintenance. Give some details of one of them.

Thistly Marsh sits between the Small River Lea and the railway line, with Bowyer's Water at its southern end. Its name may suggest wildness but the reality is pretty tame. It's looped by footpaths wide enough to cycle two, even three abreast, and passenger trains zip past every few minutes. Hackney Downs and Liverpool Street in one direction, Cambridge and the Fens in the other.

It was late September when I made my first visit. The eponymous thistles were on their way out, all fluff and skeleton. It was the same when I returned the following year, and the one after that.

Thistly Marsh became my getaway, the place where I could escape into my own thoughts and preoccupations. Away from talk of hospitals and illness. Away from the conservative politics of my mother and her circle. Away from TV quiz shows at ear-splitting volume.

Reflected light shivers over landfill. Shitty little streams pick through discoloured grass. People walk dogs and yatter on benches. In the background the ever-hum of pylons, while loudspeakers from the station announce the latest delays.

It's modern nature, a makeshift environment created by mineral extraction, suburban sprawl and municipal redesign. When I see a police diver pull off his boots, *Waiting for Godot* springs to mind. Specifically, Beckett's stage directions and how easily you could bend them to fit this setting:

Middle of the road.

A thistle.

Early morning.

Of course I wouldn't be allowed to adapt *Godot* or any Samuel Beckett work. The playwright's executors forbid any tinkering with stage directions. They insist the script must be produced exactly as written and take legal action against individuals and companies who don't follow it to the letter. I think this degree of control is absurd. Dramatic texts are inherently fluid.

Discuss the roles played by (a) climate; (b) relief and drainage; (c) human agency in determining vegetation type.

Tramping around Thistly Marsh looking for varieties of thistle feels a bit like an adult version of those school field trips. Soggy sandwiches, clipboard questionnaires, trying to avoid the eagle eyes of Miss and Sir. Thirteen species have been documented here: four sow thistles, six widespread thistles, two I'm not familiar with (welted and marsh thistles) and one subspecies (broad-winged thistle). As far as I can ascertain, none of these last three are found in Australia, but the welted thistle (*Carduus crispus*) was recorded by New Zealand's Department of Agriculture in 1911.

According to *The Historical Gazetteer of England's Place Names*, Thistly Marsh first appeared as Thisley with an 'e' and no second 't' in a 1650 Parliamentary Survey.

In England I doubt there exists an inch of soil that hasn't been trodden by a thousand human feet. Look at the waterways and thistles and feel the breath of a hundred ghosts. Feel the weight of that long history: the Romans and Vikings, the seventeenth- and eighteenth-century canal-builders, the sedge cutters and lock keepers, the fly-tippers, the trysts, the unsolved crimes.

'This River [Lea] produceth plenty of good Trouts', wrote Nathaniel Simon in 1728. 'But when it grows larger 'tis stocked with Jacks and coarse Fish, affording nothing good but Gudgeons and Eels.'

Percy Archer, author of *Historic Cheshunt* (1923), recalled occasions when freezing weather 'afforded healthy recreation on the marshes, for the ditches and surplus water have often provided safe and good opportunities for [ice] skating'.

Cheshunt and this part of the lower Lea Valley retained its semi-rural character until the middle of the twentieth century. Market gardening was the dominant industry; acres of greenhouses growing tomatoes, cucumbers and hothouse roses. After 1945 that changed. New dwellings were needed to replace those destroyed by Nazi bombs and subsequent programs of inner-city slum clearance. Nursery land was re-zoned for residential development and the area became an outer-ring London suburb. From the train you occasionally catch a glimpse of the region's horticultural archaeology. Shattered glasshouses, sunlight bouncing off broken edges.

*

My investigation into Thistly Marsh and surrounds is scrappy. I'm not much interested in the pastimes of Kings and the estates of landed gentry. But that's how the past is often narrated. While other voices, other landscapes, go unmentioned.

'No more let sins and sorrows grow,
Nor thorns infest the ground:
He comes to make his blessings flow
Far as the curse is found.'

Prolific hymn writer and man of logic, Isaac Watts, wrote *Joy to the World* in 1719. He lived on and off in Cheshunt. As did Cliff Richard and one or two semi-famous footballers.

How has the Marsh changed over time? Use small neat diagrams to illustrate your answer.

Today is colourless and apologetic. The wind hurtles straight from Siberia. It's March this time, and this time Thistly Marsh belies its name. Barely a rosette in sight. But loads of sawn-off trees and dug-up earth.

'They're clearing the way for the London Olympics,' a dog-walker tells me. 'There's a sign in the cark park.'

A public notice explains that trees are being cut down to help with the movement of people attending Olympic Games Canoe Slalom events.

The locals I speak with are sceptical. They know there are issues of chemical residue, that parts of the area are in poor condition, but it has a rich industrial heritage and they like it the way it is.

While I've been checking in on Thistly Marsh, back in Beehive Road my mother has been baking.

'I've made iced biscuits with those – what do you call them? Those sprinkle things ——'

Hundreds and thousands.

I don't know whether my brother remembers this but I do – or the writer in me does. One bitterly cold Christmas holiday we raided the cupboard for our mother's stash of cake decorations. Went outside, scooped up snowballs and rolled them in hundreds and thousands to make them multicoloured.

Mum knew her domestic science. She taught me the difference between a shallot and an onion, how to tell a field mushroom from its poisonous relative, that you should rinse wild-picked watercress with a splash of vinegar. It was Mum who explained to me, when I was living in Korea and my attempt to make strawberry jam was a runny mess, that you need cane sugar to get a decent set, not sugar derived from beet. And I can never look at blackberries without thinking of my mother. Of the miles we walked to pick them at the purple end of summer. When brambles pushed off in all directions and fields overran with knapweeds and thistles.

Thistly Marsh is thistly, but marshy – not so much. I'm assuming that once upon a time past it was wetter than it is today. That it was probably drained to provide rough grazing.

I have a soft spot for swamps, *terra infirma*, unstable zones that float between land and water where monsters lurk and quagmires threaten to swallow us whole. I regularly revisit Grendel's mere, *The Creature from the Black Lagoon* and *The Hound of the Baskervilles*' Grimpen Mire, whose 'tenacious grip plucked at our heels as we walked, and when we sank into it it was as if some malignant hand was tugging us down into those obscene depths'.

Explain a carr landscape. What are osier beds? Who or what is a pinder?

Historical research into Thistly Marsh and its environs has expanded my vocabulary. A carr landscape is a type of waterlogged wood. Osier beds are moist habitats where willows are cultivated to make fish traps and baskets. A pinder was the person in charge of impounding stray animals, and there was a pinder's cottage near the gate onto Thistly Marsh.

*

The thistles attract a republic of insects. A bumble bee like a kids' cartoon with its yellow and black stripes. Regular bees, butterflies, ants, arachnids and, according to the official literature, Thistly Marsh is a prime site for grasshoppers.

Britain's National Gallery has a painting: *Flowers in a Vase*. There are a lot of still lives in the Gallery, but I remember this one because it was by a female artist. Rachel Ruysch was born in the Netherlands in 1664 and enjoyed a long and illustrious career. Her asymmetrical flower compositions often incorporated insects. Along with its mixed bunch of apple blossom, peonies and other blooms, *Flowers in a Vase* has a grasshopper centre front.

*

Back at the Lea Valley and here's the Marshside menu: Coleman's Home Interiors; R & D Sofas Chairs and Reupholstery; Crash Repairs (Body and Paint Specialists); Network Rail Maintenance Depot; T&C Sheet Metal Works Ltd; Paddy Power Bookmaker; Cheshunt Tandoori. Self-storage, printing, wheel alignment, gym, beauty salon. Flatpacking, commuters home late from the office, dirty words, graffiti art. And The Windmill: pub lunches, beer garden, wireless internet, bouncy castle – 'Get down from there, Ashley!'

*

The day after my mother died I went to Thistly Marsh. I felt the world rush from me and I was helpless to make it stay. Both parents were gone. My brother and his family live in

New Jersey and are US citizens. What would now bind me to the country where I was born? I felt detached. I started singing a hymn I remembered from school assemblies –

Through the night of doubt and sorrow

Onward goes the pilgrim band,

Singing songs of expectation,

Marching to the Promised Land ——

The joggers, picnickers, anglers and short-haul cyclists gave me a wide berth.

My last meaningful hymn-singing was at my mother's funeral a few days later. Almost everything about that warm, rainless morning is fixed in my memory, but I can't recall the hymns we sang. Those notes are gone.

It's a sad and sobering experience clearing the family home. Our voices, our quarrels, our tears and laughter, triumphs and birthday celebrations haunt the air. But it's also revealing. Mum's kitchen drawers were a kaleidoscope of recipes snipped from magazines and packets, handwritten additions, and cookbooks held together with Sellotape and string. Recipes for old-fashioned tastes: suet crust, queen of puddings, damsons, greengages, rosehip vodka. Mum is no more and as I sift through that drawer I feel as if I'm the last person left who still speaks her language.

'It's like now there's no buffer between us and…well, everything,' I said to my brother as we tucked into the Mumbai Brasserie's chana saag and a prawn dhansak. 'We've become the frontline generation.'

The house is up for sale. In a couple of days my brother and I will fly back to our adopted homelands. July 2013. My last visit and the Marsh is in full glorious thistle. There are yellow sow thistles, spear and creeping thistles, stemless, and what I'm reasonably sure are welted thistles.

As I stand and look at those probably-welted thistles, in